DREM TO EDINBURGH

including the Gullane, Haddington, Tranent, Musselburgh and Fisherrow branches

Roger Darsley & Dennis Lovett

Series editor Vic Mitchell

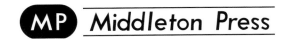

MP Middleton Press

Front cover: Class A2/1 4-6-2 no. 60509 Waverley *on the down 'Queen of Scots' Pullman train approaches Longniddry in June 1956. (British Railways/R.W.Lynn coll.)*

Rear cover upper: These branch lines were not discovered by railway enthusiasts until the early 1960s. The top photograph is J35 (Reid class B) 0-6-0 no. 64439 at Gullane station on 11th June 1960 with the SLS East Lothian excursion. (ColourRail.com)

Rear cover lower: This is J36 (Holmes class C) 0-6-0 no. 65234 leaving Haddington with the SLS/BLS J36 Railtour on 29th August 1964. (ColourRail.com)

Readers of this album may be interested in the following societies:

North Eastern Railway Association
c/o K Richardson, Membership Secretary, 7, Grenadier Drive, Northallerton, DL6 1SB
www.ner.org.uk

North British Railway Study Group
www.nbrstudygroup.co.uk

RCTS Scottish Branch
c/o R.Thornburn, Branch Secretary, 2, Tryst Park, Farmilehead, Edinburgh, EH10 7HD

Published June 2017

ISBN 978 1 910356 06 7

© Middleton Press, 2017

Production Editor Deborah Esher
Design Cassandra Morgan
Cover design Matthew Esher

Published by
   Middleton Press
   Easebourne Lane
   Midhurst
   West Sussex
   GU29 9AZ
Tel: 01730 813169
Email: info@middletonpress.co.uk
www.middletonpress.co.uk

Printed and bound by CPI Group (UK) Ltd, Croydon, CR0 4YY

INDEX

22	Aberlady	37	Longniddry
28	Aberlady Junction	21	Luffness Platform
1	Drem	67	Morrisons Haven
102	East of Edinburgh	77	Musselburgh
115	East of Edinburgh Waverley	81	Musselburgh Terminus
48	East of Longniddry	89	Newhailes
XIX	East of Prestonpans	80	Niddrie Junction East
116	Edinburgh Waverley	97	Portobello
13	Fidra Island	59	Prestonpans
87	Fisherrow	108	Queens (St. Margaret's)
88	Fisherrow Junction	20	South of Gullane
14	Gullane	56	Tranent Branch Junction
29	Haddington	XVIII	Tranent
72	Inveresk	69	Wallyford
91	Joppa	76	West of Inveresk

ACKNOWLEDGEMENTS

We are grateful for the assistance received from many of those mentioned in the photographic credits and also to G.Croughton, J.E.Hay, N.Langridge, J.P.McCrickard, A.P.McLean, J.W.Yellowlees (ScotRail).

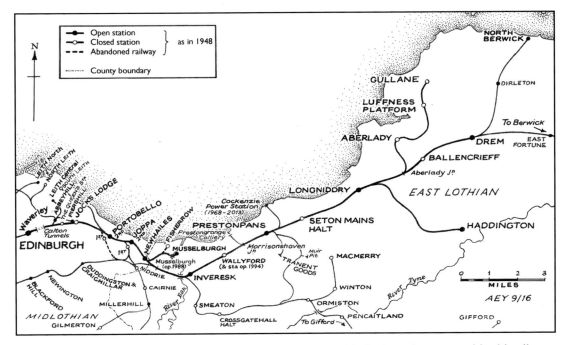

I. A map of railway lines between Drem and Edinburgh with the branches covered in this album shown in solid black. Other lines will be covered in subsequent publications. (A.E.Young)

GEOGRAPHICAL SETTING

The railway between Drem and Edinburgh runs through fairly level lowland on an East to West alignment with the Firth of Forth to the north and the Lammermuir Hills lying to the south. The Scottish River Tyne rises in the Moorfoot Hills and flows through Haddington, crossing the area in a north easterly direction before joining the North Sea near Belhaven, close to Dunbar.

The area was fashioned during the ice age, 15,000 years ago, and volcanic eruptions form hills and ridges that can be seen in the rock islands off the coast, such as Fidra.

Once rich in coal, limestone, clay and sandstone, these commodities fashioned local industry. Despite there still being plenty of deposits, coal has not been mined since the closure of the open cast colliery site at Blindwells in 1997. Today, pit head buildings have in many cases given way to housing estates or industrial development. Small harbours existed to transport goods before the coming of the railways. Coal in 19th century Edinburgh was in high demand to serve the many lums (chimneys) throughout the city and it was noticeable that the giant of Scottish literature, Sir Walter Scott, referred to it as 'auld reekie'. Today the area's main industry is agriculture, there being an abundance of arable land with wheat being the main crop, whilst market gardening delivers high quality produce which is much in demand.

As early as the 13th century, the Monks of Newbattle were mining coal around what is now Prestonpans, using it to boil sea water in large pans producing salt. This area became known as Salt Priestown Pans with the name Prestonpans emerging subsequently.

West of Tranent, the railway follows the old coach road between England and the Scottish capital of Edinburgh. Today this is better known as the A1 trunk road.

Part of the site of the current Waverley station in Edinburgh was in the early part of the 18th century occupied by the Nor' Loch. The water in the Nor' Loch, which was an artificial defensive measure, damming the streams from the west, was retained at its eastern end by a dam sluice gate almost directly below what is today the North Bridge. The old town around the castle was overcrowded and the Loch became a stinking cess pool. In the 1760s it was gradually drained, which enabled the North Bridge to open in 1772, and in turn, a new town to be built which was fronted by Princes Street. The former land occupied by the Loch was used to create Princes Street Gardens between 1770 and 1820. The railway was built at a low level along the southern edge of the gardens in order to maintain the vista from the old town.

That was the only practicable route. The Edinburgh & Glasgow Railway's 1844 Extension Act detailed the measures that the E&G had to undertake to screen the railway, although its original plan to extend from Haymarket to the North Bridge through the valley was defeated by the Princes Street Proprietors on amenity grounds. The E&G decided to stay put at Haymarket until it was assured that the Edinburgh, Leith & Newhaven Railway would extend through the Scotland Street tunnel and so give the E&G access to Leith for its goods traffic. Shortly after the E&G's decision in August 1843 to revive the extension plans, and, after several earlier abortive attempts, the hoped-for link to an East Coast company, was also assured in the shape of the North British Railway.

The maps are at 25" to a 1 mile with north at the top unless otherwise stated.

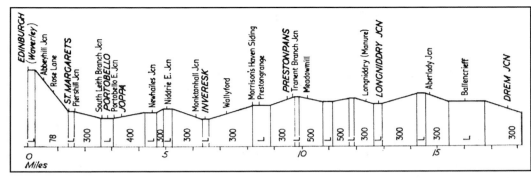

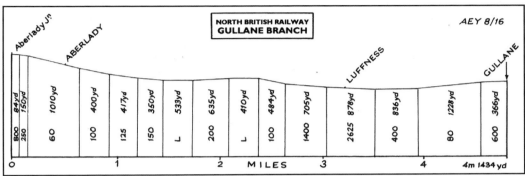

NORTH BRITISH RAILWAY
GULLANE BRANCH

AEY 8/16

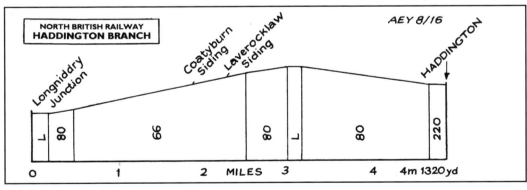

NORTH BRITISH RAILWAY
HADDINGTON BRANCH

AEY 8/16

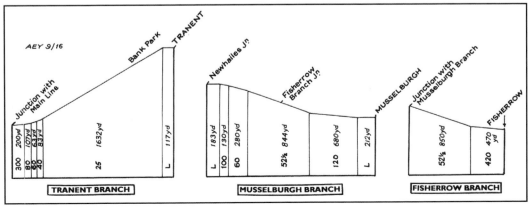

AEY 9/16

TRANENT BRANCH

MUSSELBURGH BRANCH

FISHERROW BRANCH

HISTORICAL BACKGROUND

The area covered by this album can claim to have operated the first waggonway in Scotland. It opened in 1722 and used wooden rails and horse power to transport coal from Tranent down to the harbour at Cockenzie. Its second claim to fame was that during the Jacobite Rebellion it was strategically positioned to play a role in the Battle of Prestonpans on 21st September 1745, the first ever use of a rail line for military purposes.

The North British Railway Company (NBR) was first promoted on the 8th January 1842 when interested parties gathered to consider the building of a railway from Edinburgh to Dunbar. The company was officially formed in Edinburgh on 4th July 1844 when it was incorporated by the passing of the North British Railway Act 1844 to build a line to the English border town of Berwick.The first railways had already reached the Scottish capital; the Edinburgh & Dalkeith Railway terminating at St. Leonards (opened in 1831) and the Edinburgh & Glasgow Railway terminating at Haymarket, opened on 21st February 1842.

The NBR plans failed to attract the necessary finance to build the line between Edinburgh and Dunbar. Although supported by the Edinburgh & Glasgow Railway, which would itself become part of the ambitious NBR in 1865, the scheme was seen as a local internal Scottish line and did not attract backers in either Scotland or England. Realising that English finance was necessary, the company revised its plans and it extended its line in a revised prospectus to Berwick.

Although the Royal Commission looking at Anglo-Scottish routes had favoured only one line between England and Scotland via the West Coast through Carlisle and Annandale to Glasgow, with a branch to Edinburgh in 1841, it was considered by the NBR promoters that once the railway established itself, a further route south from Edinburgh to England would follow and by building its southern terminus at Berwick, it offered future opportunities to link with lines then being built in the North East of England. The NBR was authorised by Act of Parliament to build line a from Edinburgh North Bridge to Berwick-upon-Tweed on 4th July 1844. To the surprise of many, the new line bypassed Haddington, which was the county town. Local Government reorganisation saw Haddingtonshire become East Lothian in 1921. Instead it was decided to serve the town with a branch line from Longniddry which opened on 22nd June 1846, the same day as the main line to Berwick.

The opening of the Royal Border Bridge across the River Tweed on 29th August 1850 (a temporary bridge had opened to passenger trains on 11th October 1848) finally allowed completion of the East Coast Main Line and through trains to run between London King's Cross and Edinburgh.

As part of negotiations to permit services to enter Newcastle from the Border Counties route of the NBR over the North Eastern's route through Hexham, the North Eastern Railway provided the motive power for express trains between Berwick and Edinburgh over NBR metals from 1862.

The NBR became part of the London & North Eastern Railway (LNER) in 1923. During the LNER period faster and more powerful locomotives dominated the main line express services, whilst branch and local services also saw the introduction of newer locomotives and rolling stock.

Nationalisation followed in 1948 and it was not until the introduction of the powerful Deltic (later class 55) locomotives in 1961 that enabled services to be speeded up. It was during the 1960s that the number of stations between Drem and Edinburgh was dramatically reduced along with the closure of branch lines to all traffic.

Local stations at Drem, Longniddry and Prestonpans were scheduled to close under the report issued by Dr Beeching in 1963, along with the North Berwick branch from Drem. However, the branch was reprieved in 1969 and they remained opened served by trains to and from North Berwick.

Although not affecting local stations between Drem and Edinburgh, the journey times on trains passing through the area were reduced between London and Edinburgh, made possible by the introduction of High Speed Trains (HSTs) from 12th September 1977. In 1981, the East Coast Main Line became part of the InterCity sector of British Rail.

Traffic growth resulted in two additional stations opening to serve the expanding Edinburgh suburbs; at Musselburgh on 3rd October 1988, this being the third station to carry the town's name, and at Wallyford on 13th June 1994.

On 27th July 1984, the Secretary of State authorised the electrification of the East Coast Main Line north of Hitchin (some of the London suburban services from King's Cross were already electrified as far as Hitchin). Work gradually progressed northwards, with power being switched on in the Borders in March 1991. The first electric train between Edinburgh and London (and vice versa) ran on 12 June 1991. Electrification was by the 25kV AC overhead line system. The line from Monktonhall Junction through Millerhill Yard to rejoin the ECML at Portobello (using part of the former Waverley Route) was also available to electric traction from March 1991.

Following privatisation of the railway network, subsequent to the passing of the 1993 Railways Act, services between Berwick and Edinburgh were operated by Great North Eastern Railway (28th April 1996 – 9th December 2007), National Express East Coast (9th December 2007 – 13th November 2009) and, following the financial collapse of National Express East Coast, by the Government-controlled East Coast Trains (13th November 2009 onwards). Virgin Trains East Coast gained the franchise on 1st March 2015.

Services between North Berwick and Edinburgh were operated by the ScotRail (National Express Group) franchise from 31st March 1997 - the last BR passenger operation to pass to the private sector. This was replaced by the new First ScotRail franchise from 17th October 2004, this company introducing a local service between Dunbar and Edinburgh from 24th May 2010, augmenting those of East Coast Trains in response to resurgent passenger demand. The latter service is expected to be extended to Berwick-upon-Tweed by 2018, having been approved by the Scottish Government in 2014. These trains also stop at stations between Drem and Edinburgh.

Gullane Branch

Gullane is a small town that, today, is dominated by its golf courses. These include Muirfield, which has hosted The Open Championship at least once every decade after it was established in 1891, hosting its first Open a year later. There are a number of courses in the area, including Gullane Golf Club having three18 hole links courses of its own.

In 1893, the Aberlady, Gullane & North Berwick Railway was formed to build a line from just outside Longniddry (which later became Aberlady Junction) to Gullane with a second line from Gullane to Williamston, where it was to join the North Berwick branch from Drem. (The North Berwick branch is covered in our *Berwick to Drem* album).

Although an independent line, it did have the backing of the NBR who would allow the company to access Longniddry station and use of the section of the North Berwick line from Williamston to the terminus. Authorised by Parliament on 24th August 1894, construction work commenced two years later, opening on 1st April 1898. It was taken over by the NBR on 1st August 1900. A single platform halt was opened at Luffness on 1st September 1903.

With the line now in the ownership of the NBR the route from Gullane to North Berwick was dropped. In order to generate some initial traffic the NBR purchased two omnibuses to work between the two stations, with operations beginning on 14th June 1905. It was short lived; the early buses were unreliable and it last ran on 30th September 1910.

The Government authorised the building of a military airfield at West Fenton in 1915. To aid construction, a 2ft narrow gauge railway was built linking Gullane station and the airfield site 1.5 miles to the south of Gullane. It was removed shortly after the end of the war and, today, little remains to suggest it ever existed.

Luffness lost its passenger services in 1931 and, a year later, Aberlady and Gullane followed suit, on 12th September 1932. The line remained open for freight traffic until 15th June 1964 when closure took place.

Haddington Branch

Haddington, prior to the opening of the railway, relied on the transport of merchandise to and from the harbour at Aberlady, some 5 miles distant. It stood on the Great North Road (now the A1) which linked the two capital cities of London and Edinburgh. It was a prosperous Royal Burgh some 20 miles east of Edinburgh. In the Middle Ages, Haddington had been the fourth largest settlement in Scotland. It produced high quality cloth in its mills, which were powered by the River Tyne and was a market town of economic importance to the local area. Haddington was the county town and was the administrative centre for local government in Haddingtonshire (renamed East Lothian in 1921).

Haddington was the centre for the sale of grain produced in the rich agriculture county. The branch was built at the same time as the main line and opened with it on the same day.

Much of the grain traffic, which had previously been transported through Haddington, was later moved from local stations direct to where it was needed in either Edinburgh or Glasgow. Passenger services never achieved the anticipated levels and, as a result, the double track was singled on 7th October 1856.

During World War I (1914-1918), a military camp was established at Amisfield Park on the eastern outskirts of Haddington, once part of a large country estate. The branch line services used four wheel coaches which, by then, were in need of replacement. The interchange facilities at Longniddry were somewhat spartan and, after the war, the introduction of bus services every 15 minutes during the day to Edinburgh, utilising the improved A1, saw passenger numbers plummet.

After the Grouping, a through train ran to Edinburgh on Fridays only which was Market Day. Four and six wheel coaches remained in use before the LNER introduced bogie stock on to the line.

During WWII (1939-1945), Allied troops were again stationed at Amisfield and a secret airbase where aircraft were stored after delivery from the factories was established, becoming RAF Lennoxlove; both locations providing additional traffic.

Following Nationalisation in 1948, flooding closed the Haddington branch when the River Tyne burst its banks.The service was suspended between 12th August and 13th August when it was reinstated, but subsidence on the embankment carrying the station high above the town meant the main platform could not be used initially.

The newly formed BR attempted to promote the line and also to reduce fares to match those of the competing bus services. Often trains ran empty whilst three buses an hour served the town to and from Edinburgh. It was, therefore, not a surprise when the closure to passenger traffic was announced in September 1949, with the last trains running on 5th December 1949.

The line continued to carry coal, principally to serve the mills, gas works and for domestic use. Following the Beeching report in 1963, the final closure was not unexpected. On 5th March 1968, Haddington closed to goods other than coal traffic, the remaining coal traffic being finally withdrawn on 30th March 1968.

The line was lifted shortly after closure, although the trackbed remained intact. It is now a footpath that can be accessed from the down platform at Longniddry or from the remaining platform at Haddington, which is now located in an industrial estate. The original station building remains on the platform although its 1890s replacement is long gone.

Tranent Branch

Scotland's first waggonway was built to transport coal from Tranent down to the sea at Cockenzie where a harbour had been established around 1630. It was rebuilt in 1722 to coincide with the opening of the Tranent waggonway, which used wooden rails and horse power. It was the first line to be used for military purposes when it got caught up in the Jacobite rebellion during the Battle of Prestonpans on 21st September 1745. The line was rebuilt in 1815 using iron rails to a gauge of 3ft 3ins.

In 1833, the harbour at Cockenzie was substantially rebuilt and the line extended to serve additional pits south of Tranent.

The arrival of the NBR in 1846 saw the line from Berwick pass under the original waggonway at Meadowmill. It was here that exchange sidings were developed in 1870.

The NBR subsequently opened its own standard gauge line from Bankton to Tranent on 11th December 1849, which also served pits to the south of Tranent at Windygoul. This was a goods only line.

The southern section of the original waggonway, from Meadowmill to the pits, was converted to standard gauge in 1880 when the NBR took over the Meadowmill to Tranent section. This led to the abandonment of the original waggonway north from Meadowmill to Port Seton (Cockenzie Harbour) and locomotive working was introduced on the remaining section. The old line was extended to Fleet Pit in 1900 and remained in use until closure of the last pit in 1959. Today, much of the original route has become a footpath.

Musselburgh Branch

The opening of the short one and a quarter mile branch, which formed a junction with the Fisherrow branch on 16th June 1847, resulted in the new terminus station becoming the second station to carry the name. The first was on the main line, opened on 22nd June 1846, and was renamed Inveresk when Musselburgh had its own terminus station. Trains ran to and from Edinburgh Waverley, some running via the Abbeyhill loop. The branch closed to passengers on 7th September 1964 and to freight on 7th December 1970.

Fisherrow Branch

Fisherrow was the terminus of the line from Niddrie and was built as a 4ft 6ins line of the Edinburgh & Dalkeith Railway that opened in October 1831. Trains ran from the original Edinburgh station at St. Leonards to the harbour at Fisherrow, which was the nearest station to Musselburgh geographically.

PASSENGER SERVICES

Sample timetables for the Victorian era are shown on the next two pages. Some later examples of branch ones are shown throughout the album. The table below shows the number of northbound trains before the reduction of local services.

	Fast		Stopping	
	Weekdays	Sundays	Weekdays	Sundays
1895	3	0	4	2
1915	3	1	2	2
1945	3	2	4	0
1960	4	1	2	0

NORTH BRITISH.—Musselburgh and Dalkeith Branches.

FROM ST. LEONARDS TO DALKEITH AND DALHOUSIE, *via* Niddrie, 10 minutes after leaving St. Leonards, at 7 50, 9, and 11 a.m; 1, 3, 5, and 7 p.m; (8 40 p.m to Dalkeith only;) to Musselburgh at 8½ and 10½ a.m; 12½, 2½, 4½, 6½, and 8½ p.m.

FROM DALKEITH, *via* Niddrie, to St. Leonards, at 8½ and 10½ a.m; 12½; 2½; 4½; 6½, 8·5 and 9 10 p.m.; to Musselburgh and Leith at 8½ a.m; 12½, 2½, 4½, and 6½ p.m.

FARES.—St. Leonards to Dalkeith, first class, 1s.; second, 9d.; third, 6d.

An Omnibus from Edinburgh 15 minutes before the departure of the trains from St. Leonards; (except the first and last trains) returning on the arrival of trains from Dalkeith, except the one at 9 10 p.m.

CHILDREN between ten and fourteen years of age, charged half fare; under ten free, if with a passenger paying full fare; but only one child to each passenger.

† In connexion with Coach and Trains between Berwick and Newcastle.

Edinburgh to Haddington, 8, 10½, and 11½ a.m.; 5, and 7 p.m.

ON SUNDAYS, 8 a.m. and 5 p.m.

Haddington to Edinburgh, 7 50, 9 30, and 11 25 a.m.; 3 25, and 6 45 p.m.

ON SUNDAYS, 8 a.m. and 6 45 p.m.

Haddington to Berwick, 8 10 and 11 25 a.m., and 5¼ p.m.

ON SUNDAYS, 8 a.m. and 5¼ p.m.

* Trains marked thus [*] run to Haddington.

Passengers to and from Haddington will have to change carriages at Longniddry by all the above trains, excepting those from Haddington at 7 50 & 9 30 a.m., and from Edinburgh at 10½ a.m., and 7 p.m.

Additional trains from Edinburgh to Inveresk at 8½, 10, 10½ and 11½ a.m., 1, 2, 3, 4, 6, 7, and 8 p.m. From Inveresk at 8 20, 9½, 10, and 11 a.m., 12 noon, 1½, 3, 5, 6, 7, and 9 p.m.

Timetable for July 1847.

Timetable for 1850.

Up. — Week Days. — Sundays.

Miles from Edinburgh	Fares from Edinburgh	Up.		Week Days	Sundays

INVERNESS * 584 ... dep.
PERTH * 534 "
ABERDEEN † 529 "
DUNDEE † 529 "
526 GLASGOW (Qn.St.) ‡ "

Waverley Station;
Edinburgh ... dep.
Abbeyhill
Piershill
South Leith ... dep.
Portobello
Joppa
New Hailes
Inveresk
Prestonpans, for Tranent
Longniddry ... arr.
Haddington { dep. arr.
Longniddry ... arr.
Drem ... arr.
Drem
Dirleton
North Berwick ... arr.
Drem
East Fortune
East Linton
Dunbar { arr. dep.
Innerwick
Cockburnspath
Grant's House
Reston §
Reston ... dep.
Chirnside
Edrom
Duns { arr. dep.
Marchmont
Greenlaw
Gordon
Earlston
St. Boswells 525 ... arr.
HAWICK 525 ... arr.
Reston ... dep.
Ayton
Burnmouth (see side)
Berwick 420, 426
420 NEWCASTLE "
421 LEEDS (New Sta.) "
YORK 421 "
375 LONDON (St. Pan.) "
237 " (King's Cr.) "

b Does not wait the arrival of the Main Line Train at Reston more than 10 minutes. c Except Sunday nights.
e Passengers conveyed to Portobello if room. f Afternoon Train. g Wednesdays only

Down. — Week Days. — Sundays.

King's Cross Station;
LONDON 232 ... dep.
375 " (St. Pan.) "
YORK 421 "
421 LEEDS (New Sta.) "
NEWCASTLE 417 "
From Kelso, &c., see 426
Berwick
Burnmouth 523
Ayton
Reston * 523 ... arr.
HAWICK 524 ... dep.
St. Boswells
Earlston
Gordon
Greenlaw
Marchmont
Duns { arr.
Edrom
Chirnside
Reston 523 ... arr.
Reston ... dep.
Grant's House
Innerwick
Cockburnspath
Dunbar
East Linton
East Fortune
Drem 523
North Berwick ... dep.
Dirleton
Drem 523 ... arr.
Drem
Longniddry ... dep.
Haddington { dep. arr.
Longniddry ... dep.
Prestonpans, for Tranent
Inveresk
New Hailes 544, 545
Joppa (521, 545)
Portobello 525, 544, 527.
South Leith
Piershill
Abbeyhill [532, 521]
Edinbro' [526, 528, 534]
526 GLASGOW (Qn.St.) "
DUNDEE § 529 "
ABERDEEN † 529 "
PERTH § 534 "
INVERNESS § 582 "

b Leaves at 2 aft. on Fridays. e Does not arrive on Sunday mornings.
h Stops to take up.

The up and down timetables for 1895.

DREM

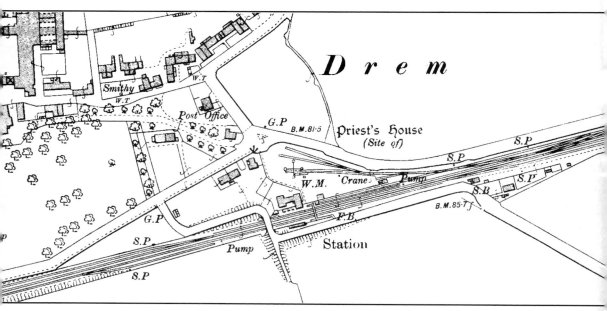

II. Drem was opened on 22nd June 1846 and was reprieved from closure in 1969. It has a small goods yard, which can be seen in this 1906 survey. The junction to North Berwick was to the east and that branch was covered in our *Berwick to Drem* album.

1. The photographer was looking east on 30th May 1914. Access to the station is shown in map II, as a footpath from the north, not the brick bridge shown below. (W.F.Jackson/Glasgow University)

2. On the same day, he took a view of the station looking towards Edinburgh. The ladies dresses confirm the Edwardian period. (W.F.Jackson/Glasgow University)

3. This view is of the main station buildings on the up platform. This time the date is set by the young lad's striped pullover and short trousers as the 1950s. (H.D.Bowtell/R.W.Lynn coll.)

4. The vans are in a long siding leading to the goods store. The water tower was at the neck of the goods yard and locomotives could fill up on the main line or from a short siding on the far side of the tank. There was a locomotive depot, which opened on 17th June 1850, but closed with the opening of the North Berwick branch in 1858. There was no shed, but facilities included a turntable.
(BR/R.W.Lynn coll.)

5. Thompson A2/3 class 4-6-2 no. 60519 *Honeyway* heads south with the 'Talisman' through Drem in the Summer of 1958.
(A.Snapper/
R.B.McCartney coll.)

6. This view of the goods yard was taken from the signal box. The water tank has been removed. In the foreground are the two steps for the signalman to exchange tokens for the North Berwick branch.
(H.D.Bowtell/
R.W.Lynn coll.)

7. With electrification came both rationalisation and restoration. This was the restored waiting room on the down platform on 5th September 2010. (D.A.Lovett)

8. A fine study of Drem signal box includes one of the ground signals controlling the exit of the goods yard. The box opened in 1918 and closed on 21st November 1977. It had 48 levers. (BR/R.W.Lynn coll.)

9. Class 40 1Co-Co1 no. 40123 heads an up express freight on 17th June 1976. (T.Heavyside)

10. This is looking east from the road bridge towards Dunbar with the main station building and several surveillance cameras on 5th September 2010. The footbridge replaced the earlier one to facilitate the installation of overhead wires during electrification. (D.A.Lovett)

11. Class 60 Co-Co DE no. 60076 passes with 6E30 Dalxell to Tees Yard on 3rd September 2004. (N.Burkin)

12. Class 322 no. 322483 approaches the station with a service from North Berwick on 10th December 2009. In 2016, the station was served by ScotRail with Cross Country and Virgin Trains East Coast passing through. (D.A.Lovett)

BALLENCRIEFF

III. The 1907 map (at about 15in to 1 mile) shows the possible site of the station that opened on 22nd June 1846. It closed to passengers on 1st November 1847, but goods facilities survived to the 1st January 1959.

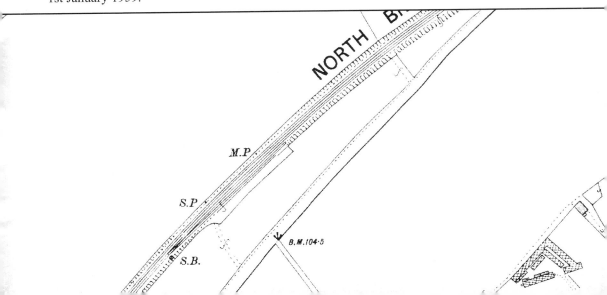

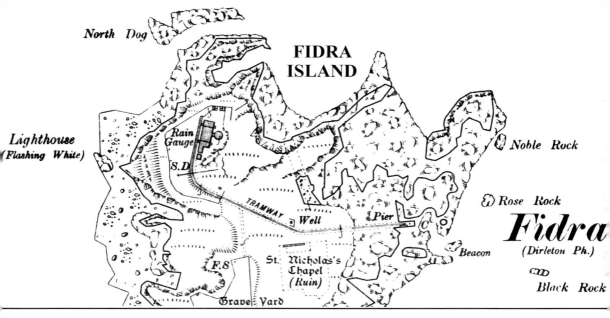

IV. Seen above is part of the 1897 map of Fidra Island, scaled at approximately 20in to 1 mile. The tramway is shown between the landing jetty and the light house. It was operated by cable and was built to 2ft gauge.

13. The tramway ran from the landing stage to the lighthouse with an incline plane. (Authors' coll.)

GULLANE

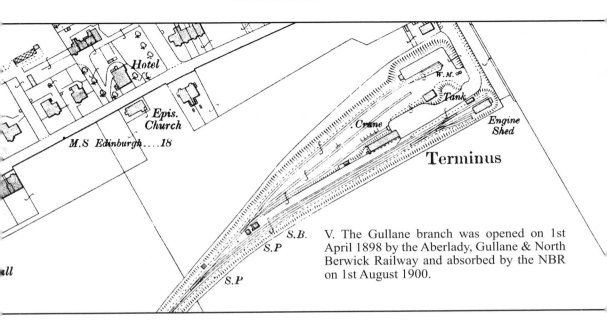

V. The Gullane branch was opened on 1st April 1898 by the Aberlady, Gullane & North Berwick Railway and absorbed by the NBR on 1st August 1900.

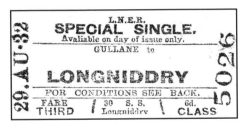

14. A short train headed by NBR Holmes Class M (LNER D31) stands at the terminus around 1912. It closed to passengers on 12th September 1932. (LOSA)

15. The NBR locomotive no. 269 is in the goods yard in June 1902. It is a Holmes class D (J33) 0-6-0 built in June 1887 and withdrawn in June 1928. Goods traffic ceased on 5th June 1964. (W.F.Jackson/Glasgow University)

16. Passenger trains were withdrawn on Saturday 10th September 1932, but occasional excursions were still worked on the branch. This is V1 2-6-2T no. 67624 on a Sunday School picnic excursion on 21st June 1958. The signal box, which opened in 1898 and had 11 levers, was closed on 7th May 1929 and from then on the line was worked on the one engine in steam principle. (W.S.Sellar)

17. J35 (Reid class B) 0-6-0 no. 64489 arrived on the SLS 'East Lothian Excursion' at Gullane on 11th June 1960. (N.Forrest/Transport Treasury)

18. The station building is seen on the same day. No. 64489 has drawn forward and run round the excursion train. The train visited all remaining East Lothian branches. (R.M.Casserley)

Gullane Engine Shed

19. This was the 18th June 1936 after withdrawal of the passenger service and the branch engine. The engine shed has no track to it, but coal and water is still available for locomotives. (W.F.Jackson/Glasgow University Archives)

The Never Built Line from Gullane to Dirleton

The original plan was for the railway to be extended from Gullane towards Dirleton to join the branch to North Berwick but this was never built. A motor bus service was started in 1905 and withdrawn in 1910. NBR motor bus no.1 was an open topped charabanc registered XS 68 seating about 20, with a driver and a conductor / guard.

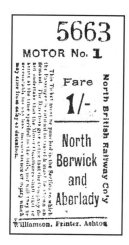

SOUTH OF GULLANE

20. The 4.08pm from Gullane passes Saltcoats Farm on 21st August 1911. The 4-4-0 is a Drummond M class, later D27. (W.F.Jackson/Glasgow University)

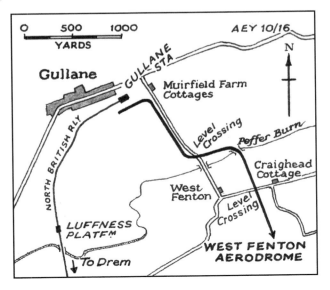

WEST FENTON AERODROME RAILWAY

VI. During World War I, a 2ft narrow gauge railway was built from Gullane station to the Royal Flying Corps airfield at West Fenton. The line was worked by 0-4-0ST Bagnall no. 2046 of 1918. The line was disused by 1920. In World War II, the airfield was known as RAF Drem. (A.E.Young)

LUFFNESS PLATFORM

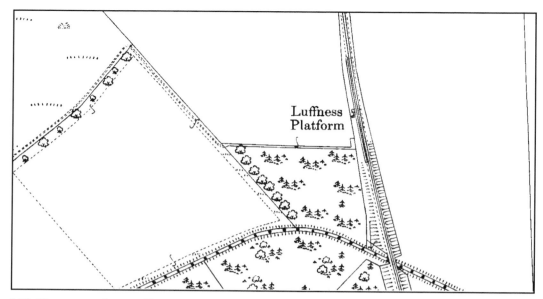

VII. There were three golf courses in the area which was otherwise agricultural land.

21. This platform was a private halt for the well advertised golf course. It opened on 1st September 1903 and closed on 1st June 1931. This photograph was taken on 13th April 1913. (W.F.Jackson/Glasgow University)

ABERLADY

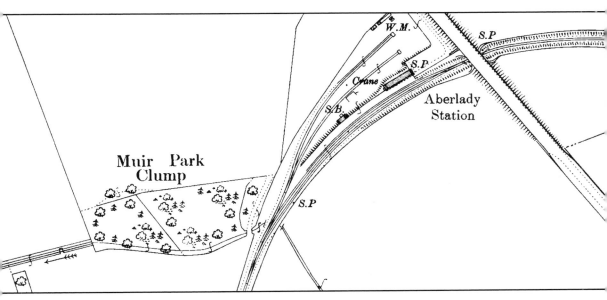

VIII. The station opened on 1st April 1898, closed to passengers on 12th September 1932 and to goods traffic on 15th June 1964. The station site is now home to a caravan and camping park. The population in 1961 was 1,172.

22. A view of Aberlady. It seems an odd choice for a whisky advert, but even more so when you see that it was for the agent in Batavia and was used locally in 1907 in what was then the Dutch Indies. (J.Alsop coll.)

23. The bridge was a good vantage point for the station photograph. The two goods sidings were behind the station building. This image was taken on 13th April 1913. The signal box, which had 17 levers, opened in 1898 and closed in 1921. (W.F.Jackson/Glasgow University)

24. The approach to Aberlady with the goods sidings on the left. The little girl in the middle of the track suggests there is no train expected! (N.E.Stead coll.)

25. A DMU passes on a special working whilst a solitary van occupies one of the two sidings of the goods yard. In the late 1950s the branch was also used for crew training on empty diesel multiple units. (BR/W.R.Lynn coll.)

26. The rear of the station from the goods yard facing Gullane is seen on 11th June 1960. The SLS special is in the platform. The station was converted into holiday chalets run by the railway in the 1950s. The buildings at Gullane and Aberlady were identical. (R.M.Casserley)

27. The former station platform is now part of a campsite, although the station building is long gone. It was viewed from the road bridge on 9th September 2010. (D.A.Lovett)

EDINBURGH, LONGNIDDRY, and GULLANE;—North British.

	mrn	mn	mrn	mrn	mrn	mrn	aft	aft	aft	aft	aft	aft			mrn	mn	mrn	mrn	mrn	aft	aft	aft	aft	aft	aft
Waverley....	6 55	...	9 c 5	9 20	1020	1033	12½c	1 45	4 c 0	4e35	515	6 30	**Gullane** ..dep.	7 10	8 13	8 50	1018	1118	1 50	415	5c10	528	6 40	9c10
Edinbro'. dep.	7 50	830	....	9 58	1045	1145	1c 3	2 25	4c50	5 e 7	552	7 10	**Aberlady** [599	7 17	820	8 57	1025	1125	1 57	422	5c17	535	6 47	9c17
Longniddry	7 57	837	9c32	10 5	1052	1152	1c10	2 32	4c57	5e14	559	7 17	**Longniddry** ..	7 24	827	9 4	1032	1132	2 4	429	....	542	8 5	9c24
Aberlady	8 4	844	9c39	1012	1059	1159	1c17	2 39	5 a 4	5e21	6 6	7 24	**Edinbro'** 598	8 24	858	9 45	....	1218	54	519	5c49	....	7 33	9c51
Gullane . arr.																									

Extra on Saturdays.—Gullane to Longniddry at 12 35 aft.   c Saturdays only.   e Except Saturdays.

July 1899.

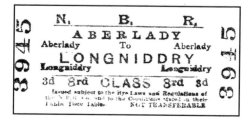

ABERLADY JUNCTION

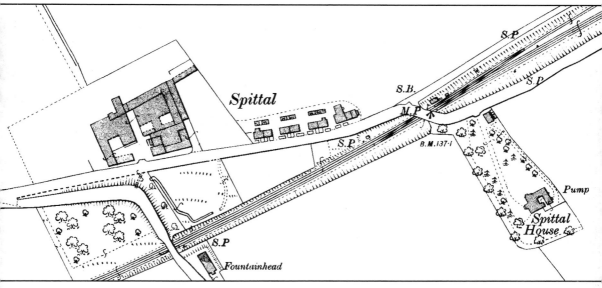

IX. Aberlady Junction was located close to Spittal.

28. Aberlady Junction signal box was tucked under the road bridge, The line to Gullane was branching off to the right in front of the box as we look towards the south west. The box opened on 23rd September 1891 and closed on 12th December 1965. It had 25 levers. (J.E.Hay)

HADDINGTON JUNCTION

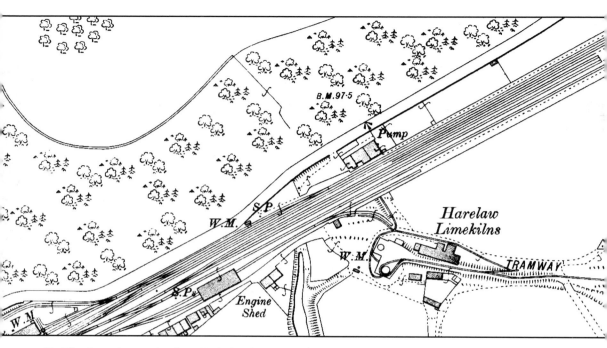

X. The branch was 4 miles 60 chains long and was originally double track. It was singled on 7th October 1856.

LONGNIDDRY and GULLANE.—North British.

Miles from Longniddry	Up.	Week Days only.										NOTES.
		mrn	mrn		mrn	mrn		mrn		aft	aft	aft	
50¼	Queen Street Station, 808 Glasgow (High Level)dp.	....	....		6 25	7 45		11 0	11 0		1 0	2 40	5 0	**F** Leaves at 1 36 aft. on Saturdays.
19¾	808 Edinburgh (Wav.).. "	6 45			7 9	9 15		1230	1F45		3 54	4 40	6 30	**g** Leaves at 5 32 aft. on Saturdays.
	Berwick .... "	....	....		7 28			1233			2 5	5 25	....	**K** Arrives at 5 2 aft. on Saturdays.
	Longniddry............dep.	....	10 0		10 0			1 0	2 27		....	5 8	7 20	**N** Arrives at 7 26 aft. on Saturdays.
3	Aberlady	7 33	8 32		9 39	10 7		1 7	2 34		3 37	5 15	7 27	**u** Leaves at 2 20 aft. on Saturdays.
6	Gullane .... arr.	7 46	8 45		9 46	10 14		1 14	2 40		3 43	5 21	7 33	
Miles.	Down.	Week Days only.										‖ High Level Station.
		mrn	mrn		mrn	mrn		aft	aft		aft	aft		
	Gullane ....dep.	7 0	8 13		8 53	1045		1 47			1 49	4 18		6 25	6 40	
3	Aberlady	7 6	8 19		8 59	1051		1 53			1 56	4 25		6 32	6 46	
6	Longniddry 808. & above arr.	7 12	8 25		9	1057		1 59			2 2	4 31		6 38	6 52	
50¾	808 Berwick	9 0		1148			4 16			4 16	6 30		8 51	8 51	
19¾	Edinburgh (Wav.) "	8 27	8 58	9 52	1138			2 59			2 36	5 16		7 N50	7 50	
66¼	Glasgow (Queen St.) ‖ "	1010		1115	2 10			5 7			5 7	7 35		9 48	9 48	

LONGNIDDRY and HADDINGTON.—North British.

Miles.	Up.	Week Days.													Sundays.	
		mrn	mrn	mrn	mrn		mrn	mrn	aft	aft	aft	aft		aft		mrn	aft
	Longniddry............dep.	7 50	8 38	9 18	10 0	Frls.	1114	1152	2 27	4 45	5 50	7 20	8 50	Sats.	1055		9 52	7 13
4¾	Haddington ....arr.	8 0	8 48	9 28	1010		1124	12 2	2 37	4 55	6 0	7 30	9 2		11 5		10 2	7 23
Miles.	Down.	Week Days.													Sundays.	
		mrn	mrn	mrn	mrn	mrn	aft	aft	aft	aft	aft		aft			mrn	aft
	Haddington ....dep.	7 5	8 18	8 58	9 33	1128	1 52	4 20	5 30	6 43	8 20		9 20			8 50	6 45
4¾	Longniddry 808. & above arr.	7 14	8 27	9 7	9 42	1127	2 1	4 29	5 39	6 52	8 32		9 29			8 59	6 54

October 1911.

HADDINGTON

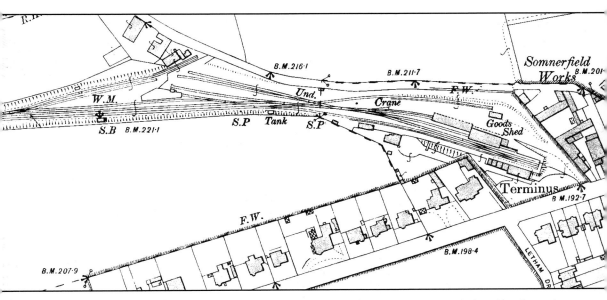

XI. The town's population in 1960 was 4,683. The town was the county capital and main grain market. The signal box opened in 1893 and closed in 1952. It had 24 levers.

29. A view of the station with the Fridays only market train hauled by Hurst designed 0-6-0 no. 1059. The original station building is in the trees and the date is around 1905. (J.Alsop coll.)

30. This is a 1930s view looking towards the buffer stops and the later station building. The NBR had an advertising contract with 'The Scotsman' newspaper which featured under the station nameboards. (LOSA)

HADDINGTON (Branch).

A telegraph station.

HOTELS.—George, Star.

MARKET DAY.— Friday.

FAIRS.—Friday after Rutherglen, 2nd Tuesday in July, July 15th, Friday before Edinbro' Hallow fair.

BANKERS.—Branch of British Linen Co.; Branch of Bank of Scotland.

HADDINGTON is the capital of the county bearing the same name. It stands on the left bank of the Tyne, and consists of four principal streets, with several smaller ones branching from it. Within the 1st twenty years this town has been greatly improved. One of its most elegant buildings is the church, formerly a Franciscan monastery. The suburb of Nungate is connected by a bridge of three arches across the Tyne. Being situated in the heart of a rich agricultural district, Haddington is an important place for the sale and purchase of grain in the open market. It contains a population of about 3,883, who return one member; two churches, the oldest of which dating as far back as Edward I., has a ruined choir, with tombs of Rev. John Brown, Maitlands, and Blantyres; five chapels; county-hall, with spire 150 feet high; town-hall, by Adams; School of Art, founded in 1820; museum, Gray's Public Library, brewery, tanneries, corn mill, four-arched bridge, grammar school, and dispensary. Here the Earl of Athol was murdered, in 1242. Knox was born, in 1505, in Gifford-street. Andrew Maitland, who married in 1657, had nine children, whose ages counted 738 years. Here prevails the custom of the bellman going round every night, singing the following :—

" A' guid men's servants, whoe'er ye be,
Keep coal and can'el for charitie," &c.

Extract from *Bradshaws Guide 1866* reprinted by Middleton Press, 2010.

31. In the 1880s this impressive station building was built with the original building becoming the station master's house. The large clock was a local landmark. (G.Angus)

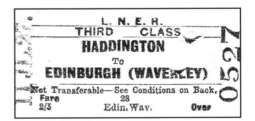

Table 172				LONGNIDDRY and HADDINGTON													
					Week Days only												
Miles			mrn	mrn		mrn	mrn		aft	aft S	aft		aft E	aft		aft	aft	aft S
	157 Edinburgh (Wav.) dep	6 50	..		9 9	1030	..	1 30	2 30	3 45	..	5 10	5 31	..	6 17	7 50	10 5
—	Longniddry .... dep	7 22	8 17	..	9 40	1058	..	1 59	2 56	4 18	..	5 33	6 5	..	6 54	8 18	1033
4¾	Haddington .... arr	7 31	8 26	..	9 49	11 7	..	2 8	3 5	4 27	..	5 42	6 14	..	7 3	8 27	1042
						Week Days only												
Miles			mrn	mrn		mrn	mrn		aft	aft E S	aft S	aft E	aft E		aft	aft	aft S
—	Haddington .... dep	7 0	7 59	..	8 37	1040	..	12 57	1 40	2 34	4 0	5 10	..	5 50	6 38	7 3	10 0
4¾	Longniddry .... arr	7 9	8 8	..	8 46	1049	..	1 6	1 49	2 43	4 9	5 19	..	5 59	6 47	7 32	10 9
18	157 Edinburgh (Wav.) arr	7½ 52	8 45	..	9 12	1133	..	1 40	3 19	3 19	4 54	..	..	6 27	..	8 6	..

E Except Saturdays
S or § Saturdays only
X One class only

November 1941.

32. On Friday 10th December 1937 the market train hauled by C16 4-4-2T no. 9449 failed to stop due to icy conditions, crashed through the buffer stops and the retaining wall and was left hanging precariously over the station forecourt. (G.Angus)

33. D32 class 4-4-0 no. 9893 is shunting a freight train at the grain and goods shed in July 1943. (A.G.Ellis/R.W.Lynn coll.)

34. Tanks of the 1st Polish Armoured Division are loaded at Haddington for transport to the South Coast in 1943 in the lead up to D-Day. They had been at Amisfield since March 1942. (G.Angus)

35. Class C16 4-4-2T no. 9451 (BR no. 67495) was at the end of the line with the 5.50 pm to Longniddry one day in July 1943. (A.G.Ellis/R.W.Lynn coll.)

36. The station closed to passengers on 5th December 1949 and to goods on 1st April 1968. The remaining building and platform still existed on 8th September 2010. These now form part of Station Yard Industrial Estate. (D.A.Lovett)

LAVEROCKLAW SIDING

XII. This agricultural area of land was known as the granary of the Lothians. The NBR built this and the next siding to serve local farms. Grain, potatoes, oats and lime were handled at these sidings, neither of which was staffed. Laverocklaw, meaning the hill of the skylark, had a more checkered career, closing on several occasions. It was 2 miles 20 chains from Longniddry.

Laverocklaw Siding

357

Pump
281

Laverocklaw

COTTYBURN SIDING

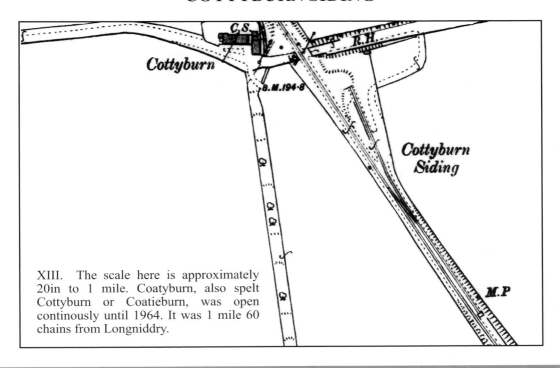

XIII. The scale here is approximately 20in to 1 mile. Coatyburn, also spelt Cottyburn or Coatieburn, was open continously until 1964. It was 1 mile 60 chains from Longniddry.

LONGNIDDRY

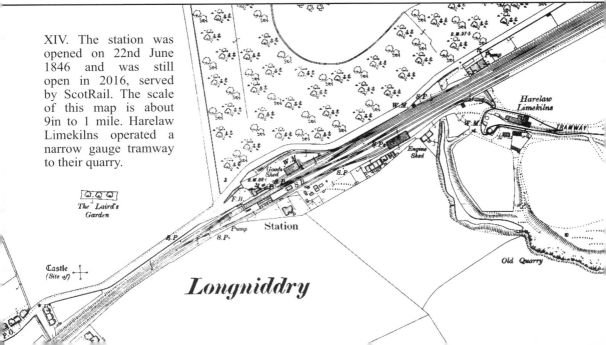

XIV. The station was opened on 22nd June 1846 and was still open in 2016, served by ScotRail. The scale of this map is about 9in to 1 mile. Harelaw Limekilns operated a narrow gauge tramway to their quarry.

37. The station is viewed from the west in about 1913. (J.Alsop coll.)

38. A class D35 4-4-0 arrives at the up platform on a hot day in July 1911. Holmes Class N locomotives were known as 'West Highland bogies' being built for that line. They were not popular because of lack of adhesion; they would have slipped on Portobello Sands! (W.F.Jackson/ Glasgow University Archive)

39. The station is seen from the east in about 1913. (J.Alsop coll.)

40. Class J35 (Reid class B) 0-6-0 no. 64489 is in the bay platform used by Haddington branch trains on 11th June 1960 after returning with the SLS special.
(H.C.Casserley)

41. Class A1 no. 60159 *Bonnie Dundee* passes through with the 09.00 Kings Cross to Aberdeen on 11th June 1960.
(H.C.Casserley)

42. The signal box was tall to give the signalman a view over the station buildings. There is an interesting signalling frame on the platform end. The box opened around 1911, replacing an earlier signal box. It had 72 levers and closed on 8th September 1968.
(J.E.Hay)

43. The Baileyfield Road siding was used by St. Margaret's shed to park locomotives over the weekend before use in the Lothian coalfield. The line up, from the front were nos 65914, 64538, 64501, 64986, 64489, 64523, 65339, 64492, 65224, 64543, 64547, 65329, 64837, 65920, 65334 and 64586. In the 1960s, the siding was used to store withdrawn steam locomotives. (N.E.Stead coll.)

44.   Class A1 Pacific no. 60151 *Midlothian* leaves Longniddry in April 1964 with the 3.30pm Edinburgh-Berwick stopping train. Nearest the camera is the down siding and, beyond that, the Haddington branch, which was closed completely in 1968. (R.Barbour/B.McCartney coll.)

45. The footbridge was replaced by a more modern structure high enough for the eventual electrification of the main line. (East Lothian Museums Service)

46. Although the line was electrified in July 1991, diesel passenger trains continued to Edinburgh and beyond. Here a HST heads towards Edinburgh on 24th February 2011. (D.A.Lovett)

47. EWS Class 66 Co-Co DE no. 66040 heads south through the station with freight on 2nd September 2005. (N.Burkin)

Extract from *Bradshaws Guide 1866* reprinted by Middleton Press, 2010.

LONGNIDDRY (Junction).

A telegraph station
Near at hand, is the old ruined seat at which John Knox was tutor.

EAST OF LONGNIDDRY
Engine Shed

48. The loco shed on 8th September 1959 was devoid of locomotives when photographed. It closed in June 1959. (R.S.Carpenter)

49. This view of the engine shed, empty again, also shows the signal box and the goods shed. The small semaphore signals are for calling-on purposes. (J.E.Hay)

Seton Mains Halt & Riggonhead Colliery

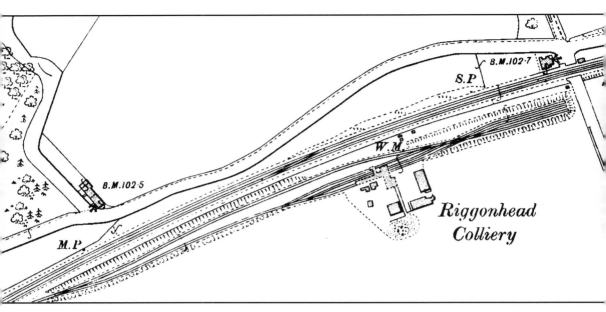

XV. Riggonhead Colliery had opened in 1897 and the map shows it in 1907. Sefton Mains Halt did not open until 1st May 1914 and was positioned opposite the colliery. By the time of the 1932 map the colliery had been closed and the sidings removed. The halt closed on 22nd September 1930, but was still clearly marked, although it was provided purely for the colliery workers.

50. Class D32 4-4-0 (Reid K class) no. 9888 passes through Seton Mains Halt with a stopping train to Berwick. The short lived station building and the crossing gates can be seen in this view. (R.W.Lynn coll.)

51. The platforms have been removed after the halt closed. The signal box remained to operate the crossing gates. (R.W.Lynn coll.)

Blindwells Open Cast Colliery

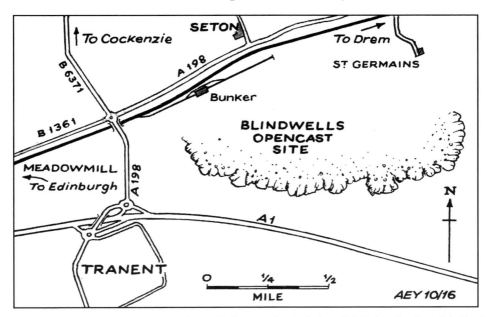

XVI. Open cast working started at Blindwells in 1979 by Fairclough Mining for Scottish Coal. 9.6 million tons of coal were extracted. The site was on the north east side of the A1, just east of the Prestonpans - Tranent junction. After coal extraction, the 80m deep hole was recovered to become a settlement of 1600 houses. In 1991, its closure brought about the end of 269 years of mining in East Lothian. (A.E.Young)

52. Class 56 Co-Co no. 56101 leaves Blindwells coal terminal with a rake of loaded HAA Merry Go Round hopper wagons about to join the East Coast Main Line in 1991. (W.Roberton)

Prestonlinks Colliery & Cockenzie Power Station

XVII. Prestonlinks Colliery opened in 1899. Its peak year was 1950. The greatest workforce was 820 and it closed in 1964. The Cockenzie Power station was built on the site with construction commencing in 1959 and the station opened in 1967. It closed on 15th March 2013 and was demolished in 2014. Planning permission exists for a Combined Cycle Gas Turbine power station on the site. The one mile branch left ½ mile northeast of Prestonpans station; see map I.

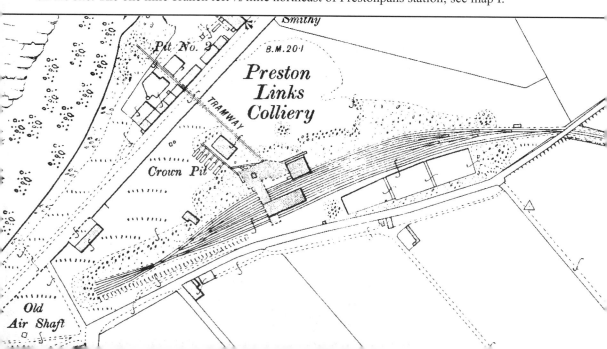

53. Prestonlinks Colliery sidings is seen in the 1950s. (J.E.Hay)

54. Cockenzie Power Station is seen on 9th September 2010. The power station was built on the site of the colliery. The conveyor carried coal from the sidings to the furnaces. (D.A.Lovett)

55. Two class 26 Bo-Bo DE locomotives are in the sidings at Cockenzie on 9th March 1987. No. 26006 is on the left running round its train having delivered coal and no. 26002, on the right, awaits departure with a rake of empty wagons. (H.Stevenson)

TRANENT

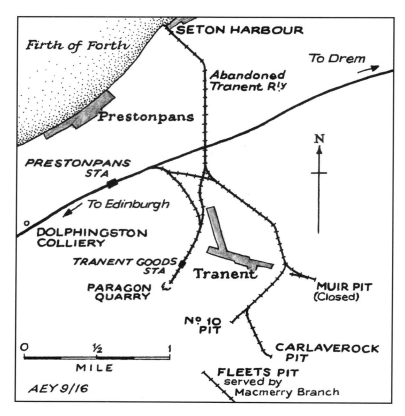

XVIII. The Tranent waggonway was opened in 1722 from Tranent to Port Seton (Cockenzie Harbour) to transport coal. The tramway was horse drawn, 2½ miles long and 3ft 6ins gauge with wooden rails and was used to transport cannons in the Battle of Prestonpans on 21st September 1745 which was the first military use of a railway line. The Carron Ironworks was founded in 1760 and took over the waggonway in 1779. The tramway was relaid with cast iron rails in 1815. The Meadowhill to Tranent section was the only part in use in 1870. In 1880 J. Waldie took over the collieries and rebuilt the waggonway as a standard gauge railway with steam engines. In 1886 the NBR built a branchline partly along the earlier waggonway. At this time the section between Meadowhill and Port Seton was abandoned. The line closed in 1960 with the closure of the Tranent Pits (Fleets1959 and Meadowhill 1960). (A.E.Young)

EAST OF PRESTONPANS

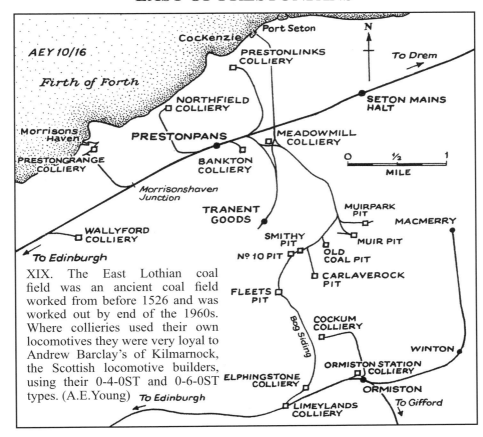

XIX. The East Lothian coal field was an ancient coal field worked from before 1526 and was worked out by end of the 1960s. Where collieries used their own locomotives they were very loyal to Andrew Barclay's of Kilmarnock, the Scottish locomotive builders, using their 0-4-0ST and 0-6-0ST types. (A.E.Young)

Tranent Branch Junction

56. Opened in 1849 the freight only branch served several collieries as well as Tranent Goods Station. It closed in 1958. These sidings are at the east end of Prestonpans station. The main line is central and the line to Tranent went off to the right. The monument on the right celebrates Colonel Gardiner who suffered fatal injuries during the Battle of Prestonpans on 21st September 1745. (J.E.Hay)

Tranent Goods Station

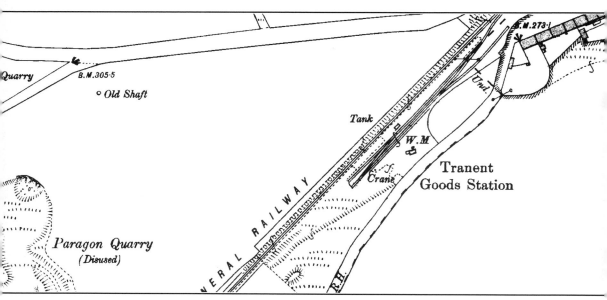

XX. Tranent Goods Station.

57 This shows the remains of Tranent Goods Station on 27th March 1959. The line from Paragon Quarry and Meadowmill Colliery is on the left. (J.E.Hay)

Meadowmill Colliery

58. Meadowmill was a drift mine opened in 1954 which closed in June 1960, but was a landsale depot from 1963 to 1970. The goods line through Tranent ended here. On 17th July 1967 NCB No. 31 0-4-0ST was stored here. Built by Andrew Barclay in 1942, their number 2146, it was delivered to the Ormiston Coal Co. It came to Meadowmill in 1964 and was cut up on site in 1970. The building behind was the pit bath house which was a late addition to most collieries! (Transport Treasury)

Extract from *Good Lines*, the monthly journal of temperance hotels (dated 1911).

PRESTONPANS

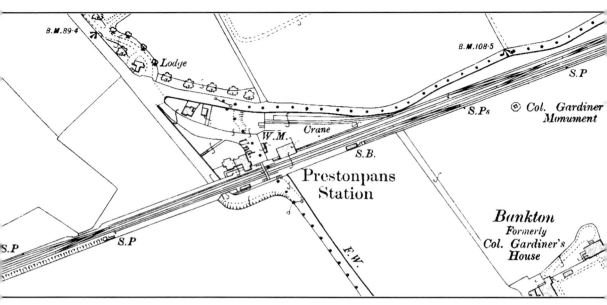

XXI. The station was opened on 22nd June 1846 and was renamed Prestonpans for Tranent. It remains open and is served by ScotRail.

59. The station sign, in this 1950s photograph, shows 'Prestonpans for Tranent' though the Tranent branch was always a goods station. (N.E.Stead coll.)

PRESTONPANS.

A telegraph station.

This place was celebrated for the battle of that name, between Prince Charles Stuart and the Royalists under Sir John Cope, in which the latter was defeated, Sept. 21st, 1745. In its neighbourhood is *Tranent*, with its Church, rebuilt in 1828, containing the tomb of Col. Gardiner, who fell at the battle of Prestonpans. In the vicinity is *Seton House*, rebuilt by Adam in 1790, on the old site close to the Collegiate Church, and *Falside Castle*, the Seton's seat, which was captured by Somerset on the day of Pinkie Battle.

Extract from *Bradshaws Guide 1866* reprinted by Middleton Press, 2010.

60. A view taken on 3rd May 1913 from further down the line and showing the goods shed, the only complete view to be found. (W.F.Jackson / Glasgow University)

61. This is a 1930s view looking east towards Drem. Obviously a down train was not expected soon. The signal box, which had 46 levers, opened in 1904 and closed on 11th September 1977. (LOSA)

62. Deltic Class 55 Co-Co DE no. 55006 *Fife & Forfar Yeomanry* heads the 08.00 from London Kings Cross to Edinburgh Waverley on 16th June 1976. (T.Heavyside)

63. The Up platform is seen on 9th September 2010 with the boarded-up buildings after the electrification of the main line. (D.A.Lovett)

64. Looking east on 9th September 2010 we have the down platform on the right. The replacement footbridge is similar in style to that at Drem. (D.A.Lovett)

Prestongrange Colliery & Morrisons Haven

XXII. Coal was mined here before 1526 when the Monks of Newbattle built a harbour at Morrisons Haven to take coal to Edinburgh. Prestongrange Colliery opened in 1829. Preston means Priest's town and Grange was a farm belonging to a religious house. The peak year for the pit was 1952 and it closed in 1962. A brick, tile and fire clay works was on the same site. The colliery was designated a museum complex on 28th September 1984. The harbour closed in the 1920s. This map edition is dated 1906.

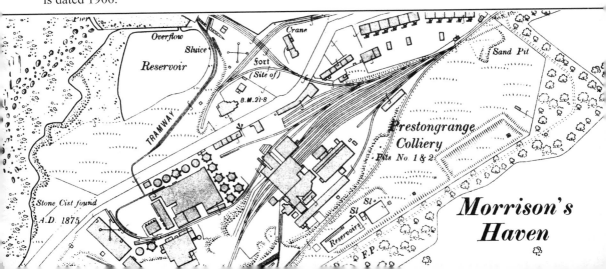

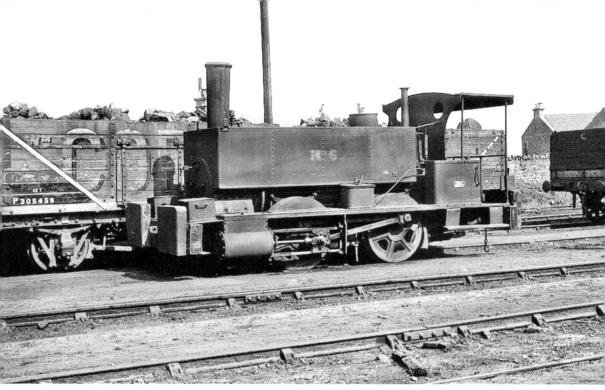

65. No. 6 0-4-0ST was a venerable Andrew Barclay locomotive. Built in 1869 it was rebuilt in 1883 and again in 1897. It seems to have spent its entire life at Prestongrange Colliery. It passed to the NCB from the Summerlee Iron Co. in 1947 and was scrapped in 1952. (N.E.Stead coll.)

66. There is not much activity in this view of Prestongrange Colliery on 14th April 1925. The barrows look home made. Perhaps their owners were doing their own coal collecting and vanished when the photographer arrived. (W.F.Jackson / Glasgow University)

67. Morrison's Haven signal box controlled the junction from the main line to Prestongrange Colliery, which opened in 1828 and closed in 1962. The signal box had 22 levers and closed on 15th June 1964. (R.W.Lynn coll.)

68. Prestonpans Mining Museum 0-4-2ST no. 7 GR 536 of 1914 works a demonstration train on 4th September 1988. The museum opened on 28th September 1984 and was operated with Lady Victoria Colliery as the National Mining Museum until 1992 when Prestongrange was recast as the Prestongrange Industrial Heritage Museum for the chemical industries, glass making, potteries and brick making. It has the last Cornish beam engine to survive in Scotland. (T.Heavyside)

WALLYFORD

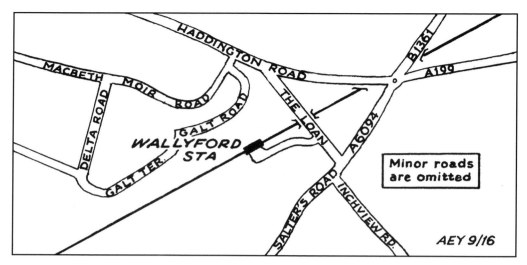

XXIII. There was no early station at Wallyford. The crossroads of the A199 and A6094 was Wallyford Toll. Wallyford Colliery was south of the junction of Salters Road and Inchview Road. Wallyford station opened on 13th June 1994 and consists of two platforms on a clear run of track with no cross overs. (A.E.Young)

69. This is the view of the station and surroundings looking west towards Edinburgh on 27 June 2002. The signal box for the colliery sidings opened in 1892 and closed on 11th November 1961. It had 28 levers. (B.W.L.Brooksbank)

70. We are looking towards Prestonpans on 14th April 2011 showing the electrification completed in 1991. (D.A.Lovett)

71. Class 322 no. 322485 pauses with a North Berwick train on 14th April 2011. (D.A.Lovett)

INVERESK

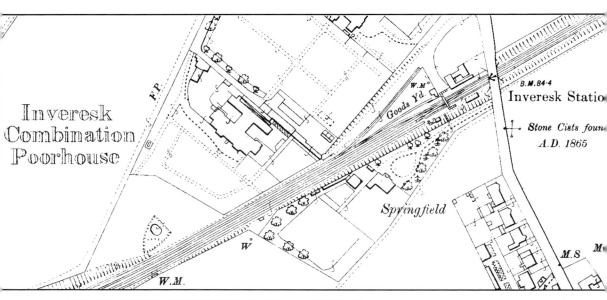

Inveresk
Combination
Poorhouse

Inveresk Station

B.M.84·4

*Stone Cists foun
A.D. 1865*

Goods Yd.

Springfield

W.M.

M.S M

We then reach INVERESK, (a telegraph station) beautifully situated in a healthy spot above the Firth of Forth, close to Pinkey, where the Scots were defeated in 1547, and Carberry Hill, 540 feet high; Fullerton's seat, where Mary surrendered to Kirkaldy of Grange, and which was occupied by Cromwell, and by the Highlanders in 1745. In the Church, which has been rebuilt, was found, in 1565, an altar to Apollo, coins, bust, &c. Close at hand is *Cromwell's Fort*, remains of Loretto Chapel, *New Hailes*, Sir J. Ferguson, Bart.; *Edmonstone*, J. Wauchope, Esq.; and *Walliford*, A. Finlay, Esq.

Extract from *Bradshaws Guide 1866* reprinted by Middleton Press, 2010.

XXIV. The station was opened as Musselburgh on 22nd June 1846 and was renamed Inveresk in 16th July 1847 following the opening of the branch line terminus at Musselburgh. Inveresk was renamed Inveresk Junction on 1st October 1876 and reverted to Inveresk on 2nd June 1890. It finally closed on 4th May 1964.

72. An overall view of Inveresk station in the 1950s or 60s. The signal box closed in 1924. (J.E.Hay)

73. The up platform buildings are complete with a British Railways sign. The station closed on 4th May 1964. (BR/R.W.Lynn coll.)

74. A1 Class 4-6-2 no. 60127 *Wilson Wordsell* stops at Inveresk on 2nd May 1964 with the 15.30 'Berwick slow'. It was the last day of passenger services. (W.S.Sellar)

75. The site of the former station at Inveresk is seen here on 26th June 2000. (B.W.L.Brooksbank)

WEST OF INVERESK

Monktonhall Junction was opened with the line to Smeaton in 1866, just east of the River Esk crossing. The name Monktonhall Junction was transferred to the junction with the line built in 1961 to serve the new Millerhill Marshalling Yard. This S shaped connecting line was electrified by BR in 1991.

76. This signal box opened in 1912, replacing an earlier box. It had 58 levers, was close to the River Esk crossing and controlled access to the line to Smeaton Junction where the lines to MacMerry, Gifford and Hardengreen diverged. A new junction ½ mile further on was created for the new line to Millerhill Marshalling Yard. This box closed on 1st August 1977. (N.D.Mundy)

MUSSELBURGH

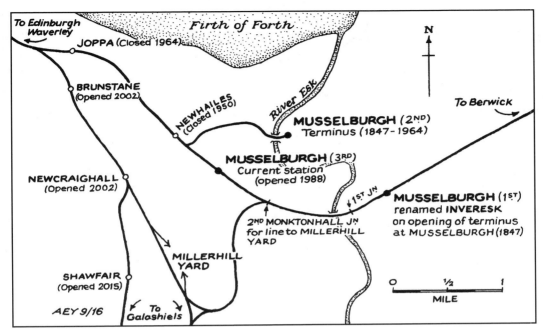

XXV. This modern map shows the location of all three stations that have served Musselburgh. The first was renamed Inveresk on 16th June 1847 when the branch line terminus opened in the town itself. The current Musselburgh station was opened on 3rd October 1988. The new Monktonhall Junction was located half a mile west of the original and provides access from the East Coast Main Line into Millerhill Yard. The up yard opened on 18th June 1962 and the down yard the following year, on the 20th May 1963. The down yard closed on 27th November 1983 whilst the truncated up yard remains in use. A new depot for ScotRail electric units is being built near to the current DB Schenker operated diesel depot in the up yard. The down yard, now overgrown, is now used for a zero balance waste depot. (A.E.Young)

Table 186   EDINBURGH and MUSSELBURGH

Week Days only

Miles		mrn	mrn	mn		mrn	mrn	mrn		aft E	aft	aft	aft	aft	aft	aft	aft	aft	aft	aft	aft	aft	aft
—	Edinburgh (Wav.) dep	5 0	5 58	728	..	8 11	8 33	1140	..	1214	1235	1 8	1 37	2 30	3 35	4 17	4 44	5 21	5 50	6 23	7 12	8 0	9 7	1020
1	Abbeyhill	5 3	6 1	731	..	..	8 36	1143	..	..	1238	..	1 40	2 33	3 38	..	..	..	..	6 26	7 15	..	9 10	..
1½	Piershill	..	6 4	734	..	8 16	8 39	1146	..	1220	1241	1 13	1 43	2 36	3 41	4 22	4 49	..	..	6 29	7 18	..	9 13	1025
3	Portobello	5 8	6 7	737	..	8 19	8 42	1149	..	1223	1244	1 16	1 46	2 39	3 44	4 26	4 52	..	5 56	6 32	7 21	8 8	9 16	1028
3½	Joppa	5 11	6 11	740	..	8 22	8 45	1152	..	1226	1248	1 19	1 49	2 42	3A48	4 29	4 55	5 28	5 59	6 35	7 24	8 11	9 19	1031
4½	Newhailes	..	6 14	743	..	8 25	8 48	1155	..	..	1251	1 22	1 52	2 45	3A51	4 32	..	5 31	6 2	6 38	7 27	..	9 22	1034
6	Musselburgh .... arr	5 16	6 17	746	..	8 28	8 51	1158	..	1232	1254	1 25	1 55	2 48	3A54	4 35	5 0	5 34	6 5	6 41	7 30	8 16	9 25	1037

Week Days only

Miles		mrn	mrn		mrn	mrn	mn	mrn		aft	aft E	aft	aft	aft	aft	aft	aft	aft	aft	aft	aft	aft	aft	aft
—	Musselburgh .... dep	5 25	6 30	..	7 23	8 10	838	9 14	..	1210	1241	1 7	1 51	2 5	2 55	4 11	4 47	5 11	548	6 18	7 10	8 0	8 45	9 46
1¼	Newhailes	5 29	6 34	..	7 27	8 14	..	9 18	..	1214	..	1 11	..	2 9	2 59	4 15	4 51	5 15	..	6 22	7 14	8 4	..	9 50
2¼	Joppa	5 32	6 37	..	7 30	8 17	844	9 21	..	1217	1247	1 14	1 57	2 12	3 2	4 18	4 54	5 18	554	6 25	7 17	8 7	8 51	9 53
3	Portobello	5 35	6 40	..	7 33	8 20	..	9 24	..	1220	1250	1 17	2 0	2 15	3 5	4 21	4 57	5 21	..	6 28	7 20	8 10	8 54	9 56
4½	Piershill	5 38	6 43	..	7 36	8 23	849	9 27	..	..	1 20	..	2 19	3 8	..	..	..	..	..	..	8 13	..	10 0
5	Abbeyhill	5 41	6 46	..	7 39	..	852	..	..	..	1 23	..	2 22	3 11	..	..	..	..	..	..	8 16	..	..
6	Edinburgh (Wav.) arr	5 45	6 50	..	7 43	8 29	855	9 33	..	1226	1256	1 27	2 8	2 26	3 14	4 29	5 5	5 27	6 4	6 36	7 28	8 20	9 2	10 6

A 1 min *earlier* on Sats.   E Except Saturdays.

November 1941.

XXVI. This is the third station named Musselburgh and was opened on 3rd October 1988. It is served by ScotRail. (A.E.Young)

77. It is 14th April 2011 and we are looking east. The bridge on the extreme right once carried the freight line from Monktonhall Junction to Niddrie West Junction via Wanton Walls. It now provides road access to the current Musselburgh station. The opening of an electric tramway along the coast from Joppa (the terminus of the Edinburgh tram network) to Levenhall on 12th December 1904 would have extracted local traffic away from the stations between Joppa and Prestonpans. Operated by Musselburgh and District Electric Light and Traction Company, it was extended via Prestonpans to Port Seton in 1909 giving it a route mileage of 6.5 miles. It closed on 25th February 1928, although the original section to Levenhall became part of the Edinburgh Corporation Tramways and remained open until 1954 and continued to serve Musselburgh. (D.A.Lovett)

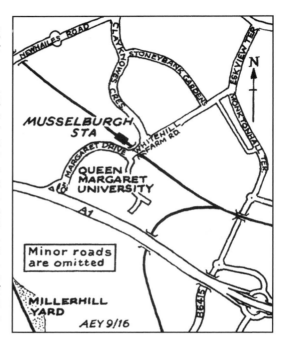

78. Class 91 no. 91007 heads towards Edinburgh with a train from London King's Cross on 14th April 2011. (D.A.Lovett)

79. The third station is located half a mile east of the former New Hailes station. Arthur's Seat on the left dominatines the skyline. The date is 27th June 2002. (B.W.L.Brooksbank)

NIDDRIE JUNCTION EAST

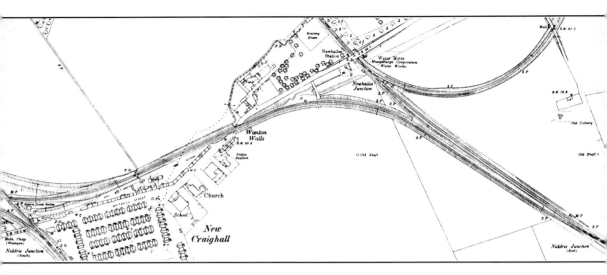

XXVII. Niddrie Junction East is in the bottom right hand corner of this 1897 map with the line via Wanton Walls branching off to the west. This edition is scaled at approximately 4in to 1 mile.

80. Class V2 no. 60951 has passed Niddrie Junction East with a down train in 1955. The tracks on the right serves Niddrie West Junction via Wanton Walls. The signal box had 16 levers. It opened in 1884 and closed in 1925. (A.Snapper/R.B.McCartney coll.).

MUSSELBURGH TERMINUS

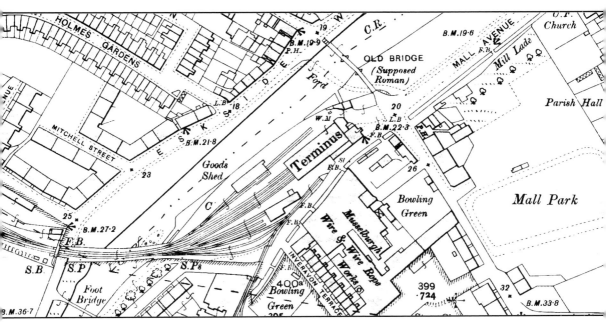

XXVIII. The Musselburgh branch terminus opened on 16th June 1847 and was reached from a junction on the line to Fisherrow at Fisherrow Branch Junction.

81. The signal box was on the Edinburgh side of the River Esk crossing. The footbridge was next to the Campie Road level crossing. (J.E.Hay)

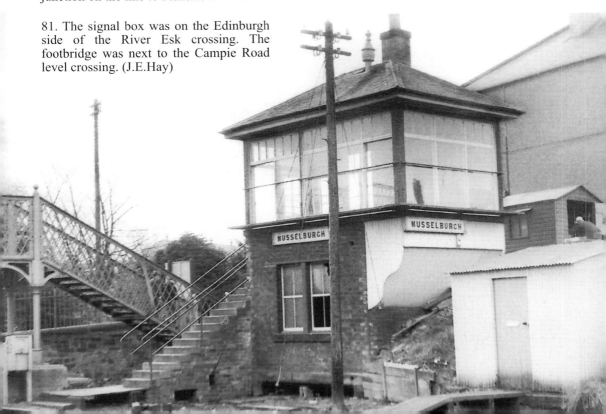

82. This was the view from the signal box across the river to the goods yard in the right and the goods shed on the left. The station is behind the goods shed. (J.E.Hay)

83. Class V1 2-6-2T no. 67609 is on a passenger train to Edinburgh while a class J36 0-6-0 is busy shunting the goods shed. The date was 29th May 1958 (W.S.Sellar)

84. V1 class 2-6-2T no. 67630 waits with the 1.54 pm train to Edinburgh on 7th September 1955. (R.M.Casserley)

85. A class 100 diesel multiple unit waits at the platform in April 1961. Built by the Gloucester Carriage and Wagon Co. in 1956, this was one of the first classes of DMU on BR. (N.Forrest/Transport Treasury)

86. The station is viewed across the River Esk in April 1961. (N.Forrest/Transport Treasury)

MUSSELBURGH.

A telegraph station.

HOTEL.—Musselburgh Arms.

MARKET DAY.—Friday.

FAIR.— 2nd Tuesday in October.

This burgh and bathing place contains a fine church, five chapels, library, bathing establishments, masonic lodge, on the site of which Randolph died in 1322, Grammar School, Lunatic Asylum, Sailors' Society, founded in 1669. An old bridge with a drawbridge in the middle, and Rennie's five-arched bridge. In the vicinity are *Pinkie House*, Sir J. Hope, Bart., Fisherow, a Roman station, Sheriff Hall, with its remains of a camp, the Links, on which in 1774, a golf club played for a silver cup, Huntley met the Covenanters in 1638, Cromwell encamped in 1650, and where the Edinburgh races are held. J. Burnet, the engraver, and Ritchie, the sculptor, are natives.

Extract from *Bradshaws Guide 1866* reprinted by Middleton Press, 2010.

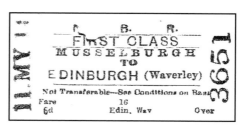

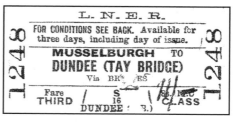

FISHERROW

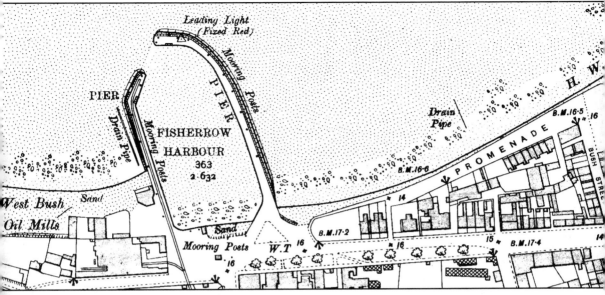

XXIX. This edition is dated 1908. The Fisherrow branch was part of the Pinkie waggonway from Pinkehill Colliery to Fisherrow in 1814. Built by Sir Archibald Hope of Craighall, it was extended to saltpans at Magdalene Bridge. It was successful and lasted until 1841. In October 1831, the Edinburgh & Dalkeith Railway opened its line to the port.

87. The entrance to Fisherrow Harbour station has a complete set of secure gates. (BR/R.W.Lynn)

FISHERROW JUNCTION

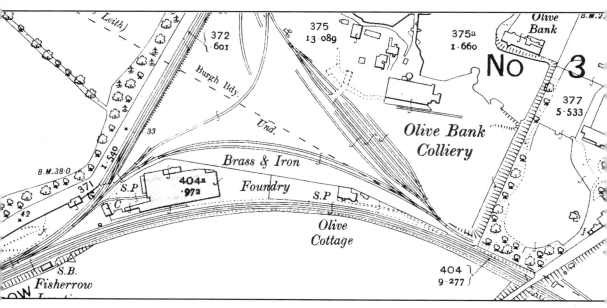

XXX. Fisherrow Junction is lower left in this 1906 map. The line going to the right of the map went to the terminus at Musselburgh. The line to Fisherrow Harbour proceeds to the top of the map.

88. The signal box at Fisherrow Junction. (C.J.B.Sanderson/J.E.Hay coll.)

NEWHAILES

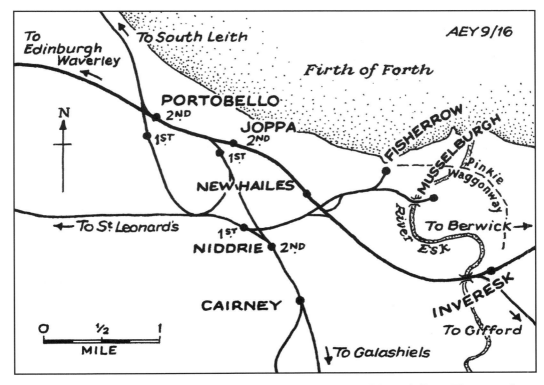

XXXI. New Hailes Junction served the Fisherrow and Musselburgh branch lines. There may have been an unadvertised stop here for the Fisherrow line. (A.E.Young)

Table 186	EDINBURGH and MUSSELBURGH																					
	Week Days only																					
Miles		a.m	a.m	a.m	a.m	a.m		p.m S	p.m		p.m	p.m	p.m	p.m	p.m E		p.m E	p.m E	p.m	p.m	p.m E	p.m
—	Edinburgh(Wav.)dep	4 55	5 58	7 30	8 11	8 29	..	12 6	1215	..	12 35	1 0	1 22	3 45	4 15	..	4 44	5 21	5 45	6 20	6 35	9 20
1	Abbeyhill	4 58	6 1	7 33	..	8 32	..				12 38	..	..	..	..	..		5 48	6 23	..		9 23
1¾	Piershill	..	6 4	7 36	8 16	8 35	..	1211	1220	..	12 41	..	..	..	4 20	..	4 49	..	5 51	6 26	..	9 26
3¼	Portobello	5 3	6 7	7 39	8 19	8 38	..	1214	1223	..	12 44	1 6	1 28	3 51	4 23	..	4 52	..	5 54	6 29	6 41	9 29
3¾	Joppa	..	6 11	7 42	8 22	..	..	1217	1229	..	12 47	1 9	1 31	3 54	4 26	..	4 55	5 29	5 57	6 33	6 44	9 32
6¼	Musselburgh.... arr	5 10	6 16	7 47	8 27	8 45	..	..	1234	..	12 52	1 14	1 36	..	4 31	..	5 0	5 34	6 2	6 38	..	9 37

Miles		**Week Days only**																		D 3 mins. later on Sats.
		a.m	a.m	a.m	a.m	a.m	am	am	am	am E	p.m	pm	p.m E	p.m E	p.m E	p.m	p.m	p.m E	E Except Saturdays
—	Musselburgh .... dep	5 25	6 26	..	7 31	8 11	..	838	..	918	1249	1 10	154	2 8	4 49	5 21	5 55	6 29	7 15 S Saturdays only
2¼	Joppa	..	..	7 26	7 36	817	836	857	923	1255	1 17	159	2 13	..	5 26	6 35	7 20		
3	Portobello	5 32	6 33	7 29	7 39	8 20	839	9 0	926	1258	1 20	2 22	16	4 57	5 29	6	4 6	38	7 23	
4¼	Piershill	5 35	6 36	7 32	7 42	8 23	..	849	..	929	..	1 23	..	2 19	5 0	5 30	7 6	42	
5¼	Abbeyhill	5 38	6 39	..	7 45	..	852	..	..	1 26	..	2 22	5 3	5 38	6 10	..		
6¼	Edinburgh(Wav.).arr	5 42	6 43	7 38	7 49	8 29	845	855	9 6	935	1 4	1 30	2 8	2 26	5 7	5 42	6 14	6 48	7 29	

January 1955.

89. The station opened as New Hailes on 16th May 1859 and renamed Newhailes on 26th September 1938. It closed on 6th May 1950. (J.E.Hay)

90. This view is to the north with the junction to Fisherrow and Musselburgh. The signal box had 30 levers and closed on 31st October 1971. (J.E.Hay)

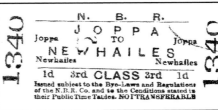

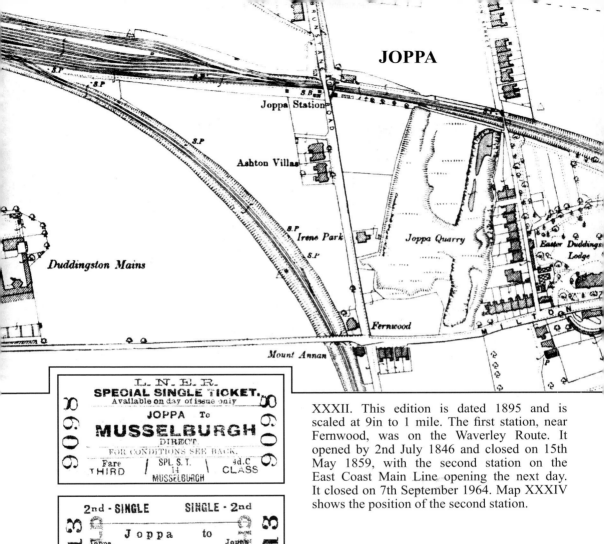

JOPPA

Joppa Station

Ashton Villas

Irene Park

Duddingston Mains

S.P

Joppa Quarry

Easter Duddingston Lodge

Fernwood

Mount Annan

XXXII. This edition is dated 1895 and is scaled at 9in to 1 mile. The first station, near Fernwood, was on the Waverley Route. It opened by 2nd July 1846 and closed on 15th May 1859, with the second station on the East Coast Main Line opening the next day. It closed on 7th September 1964. Map XXXIV shows the position of the second station.

91. A Pacific speeds through the station on a down express to Edinburgh in LNER days. The photographer was standing on the bridge. (J.Alsop coll.)

92. The main station buildings were on the north side. The start of the marshalling yard is visible though the bridge.
(BR/R.W.Lynn coll.)

93. The signal box, being tucked against the bridge, was adjacent to and controlled the station approaches only. The box opened in 1896, replacing an earlier one. It had 27 levers and closed on 31st October 1971. (BR/R.W.Lynn)

94. Class N15 0-6-2T no. 69146 drifts into the station. Like the Edinburgh station pilots, it is in immaculate condition.
(N.E.Stead coll.)

95. Coal empties returning through Joppa to the East Lothian coalfield are hauled by a class J37 0-6-0. (N.E.Stead coll.)

96. This class 101 diesel multiple unit is on a service to North Berwick on 8th August 1959. Just under the bridge in the background, a diesel shunter is at work in Portobello Yard. (A.Snapper/B.McCartney coll.)

PORTOBELLO

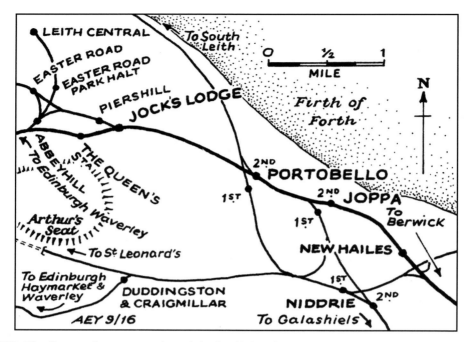

XXXIII. The first station was on the original Edinburgh & Dalkeith line from Niddrie Junction to South Leith. This line, opened in 1835, closed in 1859 and a new line from the Waverley route joined the ECML west of Joppa. (A.E.Young)

97. The very distinctive signal box spanned the main lines south of the station. The first station opened in March 1835 and closed on 14th July 1846. The second opened on 22nd June 1846 and closed to passengers on 7th September 1964. Portobello East signal box opened in 1909 and had 94 levers. It closed on 6th May 1973 and was replaced by Portobello temporary panel signal box, which itself closed on 26th June 1977. The South Leith Junction box, which was named Portobello signal box until 1900, had 86 levers. It opened in 1909 and closed on 8th January 1967. The Portobello West box had 78 levers, opened in 1909 and closed on 30th May 1971. (BR/R.W.Lynn coll.)

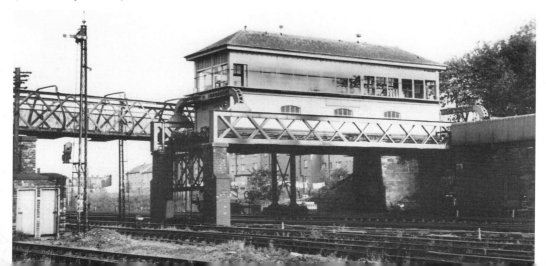

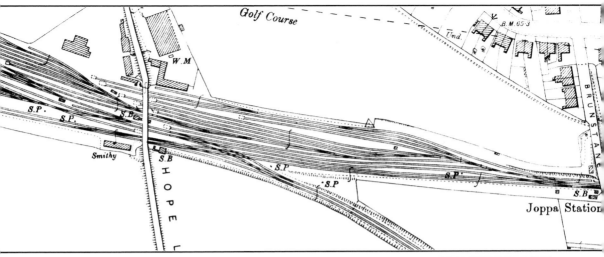

XXXIV. This map of Portobello East Junction is dated 1897 revision; scaled at 15in to 1 mile. The Waverley Route joined from the south at Portobello East Junction.

98. A North Eastern Railway class C7 (Raven Z class) 4-4-2, possibly no. 714. on a south bound train is passing through the station. (BR/R.W.Lynn coll.)

PORTOBELLO.

Telegraph station at Edinburgh, 3 miles.
HOTELS.—Commercial; Crown.

This place has gradually increased since a sailor, who was at the capture of Porto Bello in 1739, built a residence here; it now contains six chapels, bank, baths, Union Hall, glass, soap, brick, and pottery works, paper mill, and various schools. It is one of the principal watering places on the east coast of Scotland. In 1822 George the Fourth held a review on the sands, which extend about a mile in length. Fishwives' Causeway, leading to Edinburgh an old Roman road.

Extract from Bradshaws Guide 1866 reprinted by Middleton Press, 2010.

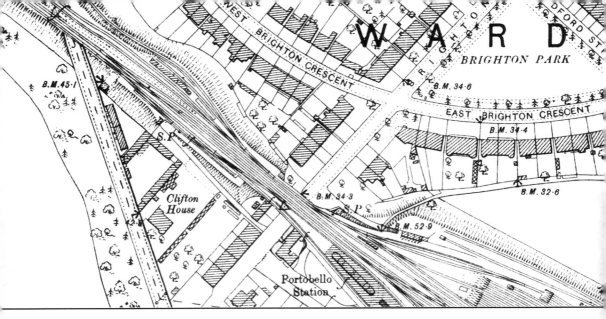

XXXV. This edition is dated 1897 and scaled at 9in to 1 mile. The west junction is a north facing junction to South Leith Docks (now known as Forth Ports). Details of the line to South Leith will be covered in a future album. The population of the town in the 1960s was 23,486. The first railway control office opened here in 1913.

99. Class J37 0-6-0 no. 64562 on a stopping train at Portobello. (N.E.Stead coll.)

100. Class A3 4-6-2 no. 60088 *Book Law* was aproaching Portobello station on 9th April 1958. On the right is the NBR engineering works and the line to South Leith. (W.S.Sellar)

101. This was the first station at Portobello and was built for the Edinburgh & Dalkeith Railway. When displaced as a passenger station it became the Freightmasters office, controlling wagon movements in the yard. (BR/R.W.Lynn coll.)

EAST OF EDINBURGH

Freightliner Depot

102. Class 26 Bo-Bo DE no. 26006 leaves the Freightliner depot with a mixed train on 16th June 1976. The terminal was opened on 8th January 1968, constructed by William Towse Ltd for £350,000. It closed on 6th April 1987. (T.Heavyside)

103. The crane unloads a train of box containers and casks. In 2015 the crane and sidings remained and an application to use the site as a waste transfer terminal had been lodged. (BR/R.Sweet coll.)

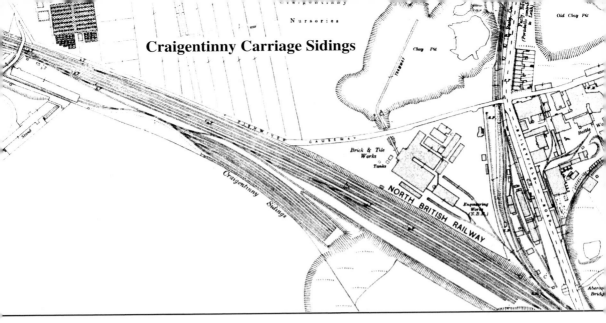

Craigentinny Carriage Sidings

XXXVI. Craigentinny carriage sidings were opened on 1st October 1914. They are marked on this 1906 map, scaled at 9in to 1 mile, the site now being home to Craigentinny Depot which looks after trains for Virgin Trains East Coast and other operators.

104. A4 class 4-6-2 no. 60033 *Seagull* is on the down 'Elizabethan' passing Cragentinny on 2nd August 1961. A class 40 1-Co-Co1 is waiting to leave the carriage sidings with empty coaching stock for the 17.15 Edinburgh Waverley to Glasgow Queen Street. (W.S.Sellar)

105. Class 47 Co-Co no. D1546 approaches Craignetinny with the 'Queen of Scots' Pullman. Craignetinny signal box, which opened in 1909, was a landmark on the route. It had 58 levers and closed on 25th April 1976. Piershill Junction signal box opened in 1909, replacing an earlier box. This had 60 levers and closed on 20th March 1966. St. Margarets signal box opened in 1868, had 30 levers and closed on 3rd May 1970. Abbeyhill Junction box opened in 1896 and was the third successive signal box here. It had 45 levers and closed in 1938. Waverley East signal box had 260 levers. It opened in 1897 and closed in 1938, when it was replaced by an LNER flat roof box, with a 207 miniature lever power frame. This closed on 30th January 1977. Edinburgh Signalling Centre was opened on 3rd October 1976 and was extended in 2007. In 2017, it was still open. (A.P.McLean)

Craigentinny Depot

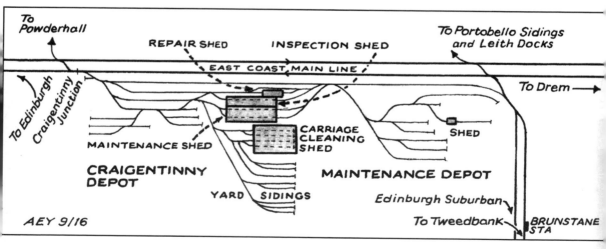

XXXVII. Craigentinny Train Maintenance Depot (TMD) was opened as a High Speed Train (HST) depot in 1977. It is in use as a depot for maintaining trains for Virgin Trains East Coast and also for Cross Country Trains under contract. This is the layout as in 2014. (A.E.Young)

106. Lined up inside the carriage cleaning shed at Craigentinny Depot, on 25th February 1996, are Class 43 HST powercars no. 43193 *Plymouth - Spirit of Discovery*, no. 43088 *XIII Commonwealth Games* and no. 43013 *CrossCountry Voyager*. (B.E.Morrison)

107. This is the east end of the depot. The building on the right is the repair shed. The photograph was taken during an official visit in July 2003. (D.A.Lovett)

Jock's Lodge

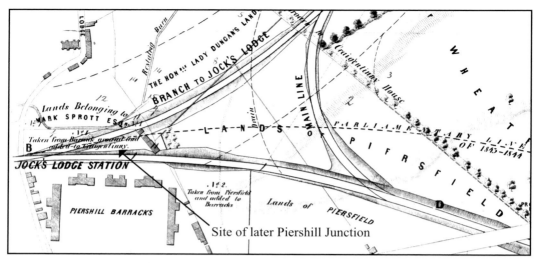

XXXVIII. This NBR map is dated 1847 and shows the proposed lines to Leith as surveyed by George Buchanan, Civil Engineer, Edinburgh. The station closed in 1847 and is marked here to be opposite Piershill Barracks. Map XL, on the next page, also shows the Barracks, with St. Margaret's Works being to the left and not shown on the map. The junctions took a different form when built.

QUEENS (ST. MARGARET'S)

A short lived station on the site of St Margaret's was built for Queen Victoria who used it when visiting Holyrood Palace en-route to Balmoral. It opened on 29th August 1850 and closed on 23rd August 1867. It was rebuilt and reopened on 14th August 1872 and was last used by the Queen on 26th August 1881. It was reportedly used on 27th December 1883 to transfer 10 convicts from Calton Jail to Edinburgh Waverley where their special coach was put on an up express to London, their final destination being Chatham.

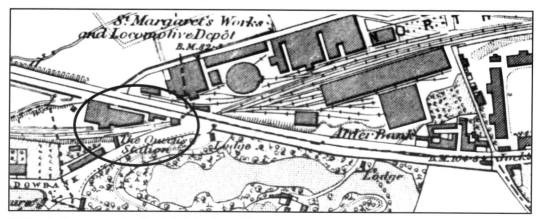

XXXIX. Queens station is highlighted on this 1877 map at 6ins to a mile. St. Margaret's engine sheds can be seen on the right.

St. Margaret's Shed & Works

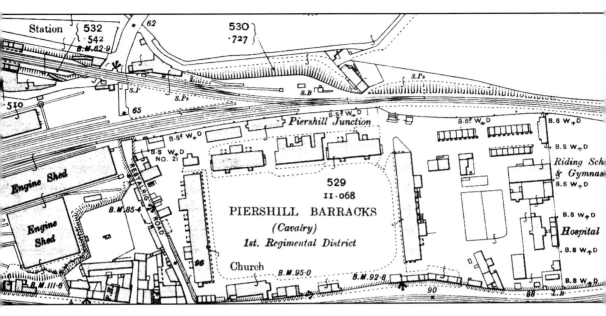

XL. We travel from the right of the map above and continue on the top-right of the one below. The works was built in 1846 as the NBR's central workshops. 33 locomotives were built here between 1856 and 1859. In the 1860s, the main works was moved to Glasgow and St Margaret's became a major shed but did light repairs and intermediate repairs until 1925. After that date it only carried out light and running repairs.

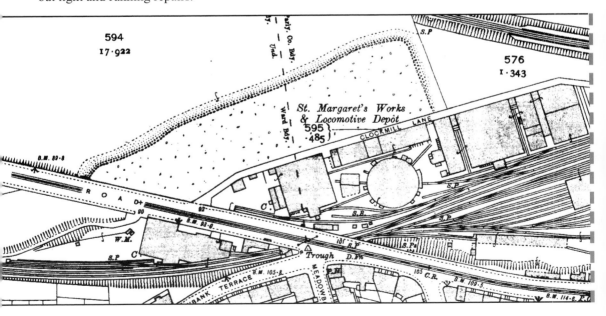

108. An interesting view of part of St Margaret's works in NBR times. The three locomotives are 0-6-0Ts that later became J83 and J88 classes in LNER and BR days. (R.W.Lynn coll.)

109. The roundhouse was on the north side in 1846. In the 1860s the NBR built a six road shed on the south side. The North Eastern Railway opened a shed in 1871 after the 1869 agreement to allow the NER access to Edinburgh. In 1923 the sheds became one unit under the LNER. It closed on 1st May 1967. On 20th June 1949, class J88 0-6-0T no. 68334 stands outside St. Margaret's works offices. The J88 was a Reid class F design with a short wheelbase. No. 68334 was built in March 1909 and saw 50 years use, being withdrawn in June 1959. (H.C.Casserley)

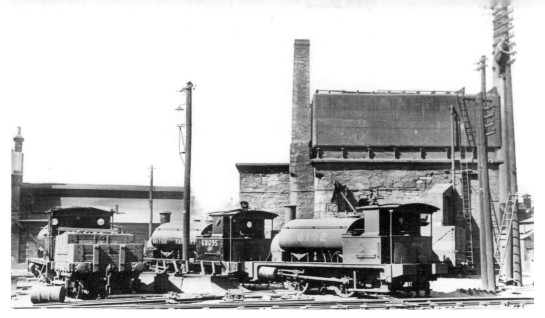

110. On 20th June 1949, three NBR 'Pugs' were on the turntable. The Caledonian Railway had similar locomotives that were useful in docks railways. These Y9 class 0-4-0ST were a Holmes design of 1882 and were often paired with a wooden tender. No. 68095 has been preserved. (H.C.Casserley)

111. St Margaret's was an old works and repairs were often under very primitive conditions. On the 14th August 1955 class Y9 0-4-0ST no. 68118 was having its driving wheels removed. (W.S.Sellar)

112. The main shed was also visited on 20th June 1949. From left to right are a J24 class 0-6-0, a War Department class 2-8-0, a class J37 0-6-0 and a V1 class 2-6-2T. A Caledonian Railway Class 60 4-6-0 stands in front of the J24. (H.C.Casserley)

113. St Margaret's shed was either side of the main line and was a very smokey shed. On 17th September 1949, a class Y9 0-4-0ST is moving off shed. Other locomotives at the coaling stage are under the smoke haze. St. Margaret's signal box, on the left, was a high box on a 'stalk'. (R.W.Lynn coll.)

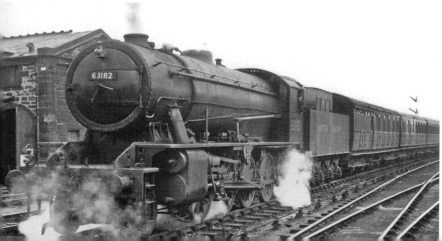

114. This is an unusual picture. Ex War Department class 2-8-0 (LNER class O7) no. 63182 heads towards Waverley with a local train. An unusual working as the locomotive is displaying the express meat or fish head-code. (B.W.L.Brooksbank)

EAST OF EDINBURGH WAVERLEY

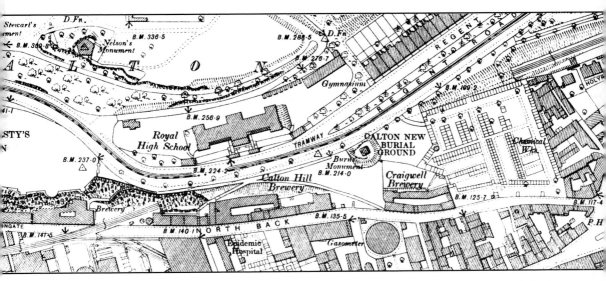

XLI. The 1897 map, at 15in to 1 mile shows the two portals of Calton Tunnel and, on the left, the eastern end of Edinburgh Waverley station.

115. Emerging from Calton North portal is an unidentified A1 class 4-6-2 working the 3.30pm SX Edinburgh to Berwick stopper and was one of the last regular Pacific workings in the early 1960s. The three carriages originated from Corstorphine, latterly as the 2.42pm SX from there, which was previously an empty stock working. (A.P.McLean)

EDINBURGH WAVERLEY

116. The panorama is from 1914 with Drummond R class (D51) 4-4-0T no. 98 piloting Reid M class (G9) 0-4-4T no. 353, on a train from Musselburgh. Another M class (G9) 0-4-4T no. 354 is station pilot. In the background is the former Calton prison. (R.W.Lynn coll.)

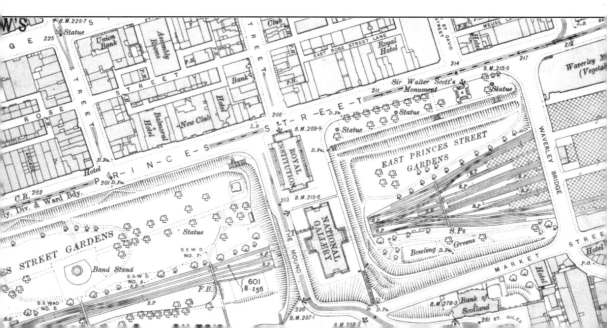

EDINBURGH, so called from Edwin, king of Northumbria, who built a castle here in the seventh century, while others claim the origin from the two Gaelic words, "*Dun Edin*," which signifies "*the face of a hill*." It covers a space of from two to two and a half miles square, and contains the old town on the east between the Castle, Holyrood Palace, and the Abbey; the south town, round Heriot's Hospital, Newington, and Morningside; and the new town on the north and north-west. Both the south and new towns have been erected within the last hundred years; the latter especially, comprises many noble streets and squares, built of the beautiful stone from Craigleith quarry (two miles distant from the city). In the old town, along the High from the city). In the old town, along the High Street, Canongate, Grassmarket, &c., many houses are of Queen Mary's time, divided by narrow dark closes (or alleys), and from six to ten stories (or flats) high. Between it and the new town are east and west Princes Street Gardens, beautifully laid out, and through which the Edinburgh and Glasgow, and North British railways pass; this was formerly called the North or Nor' Loch, a sheet of stagnant water; there are the North and Waverley bridges, and Mound, forming a connection with the old and new town. Of the numerous fine structures which adorn the "Modern Athens," as it has been styled from a similarity in its general appearance.

Extract from *Bradshaws Guide 1866* reprinted by Middleton Press, 2010.

XLII. On opening, the line from Berwick ended initially at Physic Gardents and then North Bridge. A new joint station between the NBR and the Edinburgh & Glasgow Railway was called Waverley Bridge and opened on 28th February 1848, though the NBR used some facilities from the 17th May 1847. The Canal Street terminus of the Edinburgh, Leith & Granton Railway also opened on that day. The name of Waverley Bridge was soon abbreviated to Waverley, and the whole complex came under the NBR in 1865. The station was rebuilt between 1890 and 1900. The North British Hotel opened on 16th October 1902. The station was renamed Edinburgh, dropping the Waverley suffix on 18th April 1966. A new travel centre opened on 6th July 1976.

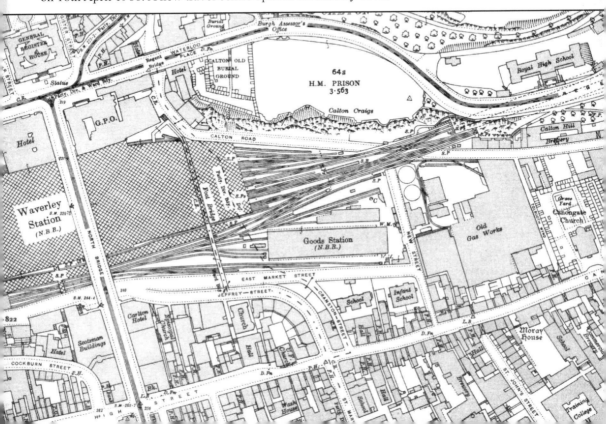

117. 4-4-2 no. 875 *Midlothian is* leaving Edinburgh Waverley with a southbound express in NBR days. (J.Alsop coll.)

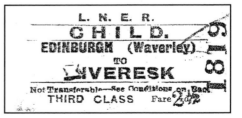

118. Class 55 Deltic Co-CoDE no. D9004 *Queen's Own Highlander* is leaving Waverley on 1st June 1961 with the 'Flying Scotsman'. This was the first day of its Deltic haulage. (W.S.Sellar)

119. This view of Waverley station is from 2014. In the foreground a class 170 DMU is entering the station. An HST is about to depart south. New buildings to the left of the tracks occupy the site of the former goods yard. (D.A.Lovett)

120. CrossCountry class 221 Super Voyager no. 221130 arrives from the south, drawing alongside class 380 no. 380106 on 12th July 2011. A major restoration project for the station was completed in 2014 and included reglazing of the station roof and replacing Waverley steps with escalators in 2011. These improvements brought light and comfort to the station. (R.R.Darsley)

MP Middleton Press

EVOLVING THE ULTIMATE RAIL ENCYCLOPEDIA

Easebourne Midhurst GU29 9AZ. Tel:01730 813169

www.middletonpress.co.uk email:info@middletonpress.co.uk
A-978 0 906520 B- 978 1 873793 C- 978 1 901706 D-978 1 904474
E - 978 1 906008 F - 978 1 908174 G -978 1 910356

A

Abergavenny to Merthyr C 91 8
Abertillery & Ebbw Vale Lines D 84 5
Aberystwyth to Carmarthen E 90 1
Allhallows - Branch Line to A 62 8
Alton - Branch Lines to A 11 6
Andover to Southampton A 82 6
Ascot - Branch Lines around A 64 2
Ashburton - Branch Line to B 95 4
Ashford - Steam to Eurostar B 67 1
Ashford to Dover A 48 2
Austrian Narrow Gauge D 04 3
Avonmouth - BL around D 42 5
Aylesbury to Rugby D 91 3

B

Baker Street to Uxbridge D 90 6
Bala to Llandudno E 87 1
Banbury to Birmingham D 27 2
Banbury to Cheltenham E 63 5
Bangor to Holyhead F 01 7
Bangor to Portmadoc E 72 7
Barking to Southend C 80 2
Barmouth to Pwllheli E 53 6
Barry - Branch Lines around D 50 0
Bartlow - Branch Lines to F 27 7
Bath Green Park to Bristol C 36 9
Bath to Evercreech Junction A 60 4
Beamish 40 years on rails E94 9
Bedford to Wellingborough D 31 9
Berwick to Drem F 64 2
Berwick to St. Boswells F 75 8
B'ham to Tamworth & Nuneaton F 63 5
Birkenhead to West Kirby F 61 1
Birmingham to Wolverhampton E253
Blackburn to Hellifield F 95 6
Bletchley to Cambridge D 94 4
Bletchley to Rugby E 07 9
Bodmin - Branch Lines around B 83 1
Boston to Lincoln F 80 2
Bournemouth to Evercreech Jn A 46 8
Bournemouth to Weymouth A 57 4
Bradshaw's History F 15 7
Bradshaw's Rail Times 1850 F 13 0
Bradshaw's Rail Times 1895 F 11 6
Branch Lines series - see town names
Brecon to Neath D 43 2
Brecon to Newport D 16 6
Brecon to Newtown E 06 2
Brighton to Eastbourne A 16 1
Brighton to Worthing A 03 1
Bristol to Taunton D 03 6
Bromley South to Rochester B 23 7
Bromsgrove to Birmingham D 87 6
Bromsgrove to Gloucester D 73 9
Broxbourne to Cambridge F16 1
Brunel - A railtour D 74 6
Bude - Branch Line to B 29 9
Burnham to Evercreech Jn B 68 0

C

Cambridge to Ely D 55 5
Canterbury - BLs around B 58 9
Cardiff to Dowlais (Cae Harris) F 47 5
Cardiff to Pontypridd E 95 6
Cardiff to Swansea E 42 0
Carlisle to Hawick E 85 7
Carmarthen to Fishguard E 66 6
Caterham & Tattenham Corner B251
Central & Southern Spain NG E 91 8
Chard and Yeovil - BLs a C 30 7
Charing Cross to Dartford A 75 8
Charing Cross to Orpington A 96 3
Cheddar - Branch Line to B 90 9
Cheltenham to Andover C 43 7
Cheltenham to Redditch D 81 4
Chester to Birkenhead F 21 5
Chester to Manchester F 51 2
Chester to Rhyl E 93 2
Chester to Warrington F 40 6
Clacton and Walton - BLs to F 04 8
Clapham Jn to Beckenham Jn B 36 7
Cleobury Mortimer - BLs a E 18 5

Clevedon & Portishead - BLs to D180
Consett to South Shields E 57 4
Cornwall Narrow Gauge D 56 2
Corris and Vale of Rheidol E 65 9
Coventry to Leicester G 00 5
Craven Arms to Llandeilo E 35 2
Craven Arms to Wellington E 33 8
Crawley to Littlehampton A 34 5
Crewe to Manchester F 57 4
Cromer - Branch Lines around C 26 0
Croydon to East Grinstead B 48 0
Crystal Palace & Catford Loop B 87 1
Cyprus Narrow Gauge E 13 0

D

Darjeeling Revisited F 09 3
Darlington Leamside Newcastle E 28 4
Darlington to Newcastle D 98 2
Denbigh - Branch Lines around F 32 1
Derby to Stoke-on-Trent F 93 2
Derwent Valley - BL to the D 06 7
Devon Narrow Gauge E 09 3
Didcot to Banbury D 02 9
Didcot to Swindon C 84 0
Didcot to Winchester C 13 0
Dorset & Somerset NG D 76 0
Douglas - Laxey - Ramsey E 75 8
Douglas to Peel C 88 8
Douglas to Port Erin C 55 0
Douglas to Ramsey D 39 5
Dover to Ramsgate A 78 9
Drem to Edinburgh G 06 7
Dublin Northwards in 1950s E 31 4
Dunstable - Branch Lines to E 27 7

E

Ealing to Slough C 42 0
Eastbourne to Hastings A 27 7
East Cornwall Mineral Railways D 22 7
East Croydon to Three Bridges A 53 8
Eastern Spain Narrow Gauge E 56 7
East Grinstead - BLs to A 07 9
East Kent Light Railway A 61 1
East London - Branch Lines of C 44 4
East London Line B 80 0
East of Norwich - Branch Lines E 69 7
Effingham Junction - BLs a A 74 1
Ely to Norwich C 90 1
Enfield Town & Palace Gates D 32 6
Epsom to Horsham A 30 7
Eritrean Narrow Gauge E 38 3
Euston to Harrow & Wealdstone C 89 5
Exeter to Barnstaple B 15 2
Exeter to Newton Abbot C 49 9
Exeter to Tavistock B 69 5
Exmouth - Branch Lines to B 00 8

F

Fairford - Branch Line to A 52 9
Falmouth, Helston & St. Ives C 74 1
Fareham to Salisbury A 67 3
Faversham to Dover B 05 3
Felixstowe & Aldeburgh - BL to D 20 3
Fenchurch Street to Barking C 20 8
Festiniog - 50 yrs of enterprise C 83 3
Festiniog 1946-55 E 01 7
Festiniog in the Fifties B 68 8
Festiniog in the Sixties B 91 6
Ffestiniog in Colour 1955-82 F 25 3
Finsbury Park to Alexandra Pal C 02 8
French Metre Gauge Survivors F 88 8
Frome to Bristol B 77 0

G

Galashiels to Edinburgh F 52 9
Gloucester to Bristol D 35 7
Gloucester to Cardiff D 66 1
Gosport - Branch Lines around A 36 9
Greece Narrow Gauge D 72 2

H

Hampshire Narrow Gauge D 36 4
Harrow to Watford D 14 2
Harwich & Hadleigh - BLs to F 02 4
Harz Revisited F 62 8

Hastings to Ashford A 37 6
Hawick to Galashiels F 36 9
Hawkhurst - Branch Line to A 66 6
Hayling - Branch Line to A 12 3
Hay-on-Wye - BL around D 92 0
Haywards Heath to Seaford A 28 4
Hemel Hempstead - BLs to D 88 3
Henley, Windsor & Marlow - BLa C77 2
Hereford to Newport D 54 8
Hertford & Hatfield - BLs a E 58 1
Hertford Loop E 71 0
Hexham to Carlisle D 75 3
Hexham to Hawick F 08 6
Hitchin to Peterborough D 07 4
Holborn Viaduct to Lewisham A 81 9
Horsham - Branch Lines to A 02 4
Huntingdon - Branch Line to A 93 2

I

Ilford to Shenfield C 97 0
Ilfracombe - Branch Line to B 21 3
Industrial Rlys of the South East A 09 3
Ipswich to Diss F 81 9
Ipswich to Saxmundham C 41 3
Isle of Man Railway Journey G 02 9
Isle of Wight Lines - 50 yrs C 12 3
Italy Narrow Gauge F 17 8

K

Kent Narrow Gauge C 45 1
Kettering to Nottingham F 82-6
Kidderminster to Shrewsbury E 10 9
Kingsbridge - Branch Line to C 98 7
Kings Cross to Potters Bar E 62 8
King's Lynn to Hunstanton F 58 1
Kingston & Hounslow Loops A 83 3
Kingswear - Branch Line to C 17 8

L

Lambourn - Branch Line to C 70 3
Launceston & Princetown - BLs C 19 2
Leek - Branch Line From G 01 2
Leicester to Burton F 85 7
Lewisham to Dartford A 92 5
Lincoln to Cleethorpes F 56 7
Lincoln to Doncaster G 03 6
Lines around Stamford F 98 7
Lines around Wimbledon B 75 6
Liverpool Street to Chingford D 01 2
Liverpool Street to Ilford C 34 5
Llandeilo to Swansea E 46 8
London Bridge to Addiscombe B 20 6
London Bridge to East Croydon A 58 1
Longmoor - Branch Lines to A 41 3
Looe - Branch Line to C 22 2
Loughborough to Nottingham F 82 4
Lowestoft - BLs around E 40 6
Ludlow to Hereford E 14 7
Lydney - Branch Lines around E 26 0
Lyme Regis - Branch Line to A 45 1
Lynton - Branch Line to B 04 6

M

Machynlleth to Barmouth E 54 3
Maesteg and Tondu Lines E 06 2
Majorca & Corsica Narrow Gauge F 41 3
March - Branch Lines around B 09 1
Market Drayton - BLs around F 67 3
Market Harborough to Newark F 86 4
Marylebone to Rickmansworth D 49 4
Melton Constable to Yarmouth Bch E031
Midhurst - Branch Lines of E 78 9
Midhurst - Branch Lines to F 00 0
Minehead - Branch Line to A 80 2
Mitcham Junction Lines B 01 5
Monmouth - Branch Lines to E 20 8
Monmouthshire Eastern Valleys D 71 5
Moretonhampstead - BL to C 27 7
Moreton-in-Marsh to Worcester D 26 5
Morpeth to Bellingham F 87 1
Mountain Ash to Neath D 80 7

N

Newark to Doncaster F 78 9
Newbury to Westbury C 66 6
Newcastle to Hexham D 69 2

Newport (IOW) - Branch Lines to A 26 0
Newquay - Branch Lines to C 71 0
Newton Abbot to Plymouth C 60 4
Newtown to Aberystwyth E 41 3
Northampton to Peterborough F 92 5
North East German NG D 44 9
Northern Alpine Narrow Gauge F 37 6
Northern France Narrow Gauge C 75 8
Northern Spain Narrow Gauge E 83 3
North London Line B 94 7
North of Birmingham F 55 0
Nottingham to Boston F 70 3
Nottingham to Lincoln F 43 7

O

Ongar - Branch Line to E 05 5
Orpington to Tonbridge B 03 9
Oswestry - Branch Lines around E 60 4
Oswestry to Whitchurch E 81 9
Oxford to Bletchley D 57 9
Oxford to Moreton-in-Marsh D 15 9

P

Paddington to Ealing C 37 6
Paddington to Princes Risborough C819
Padstow - Branch Line to B 54 1
Pembroke and Cardigan - BLs to F 29 1
Peterborough to Kings Lynn E 32 1
Peterborough to Lincoln F 89 5
Peterborough to Newark F 72 7
Plymouth - BLs around B 98 5
Plymouth to St. Austell C 63 5
Pontypool to Mountain Ash D 65 4
Pontypridd to Merthyr F 14 7
Pontypridd to Port Talbot E 86 4
Porthmadog 1954-94 - BLa B 31 2
Portmadoc 1923-46 - BLa B 13 8
Portsmouth to Southampton A 31 4
Portugal Narrow Gauge E 67 3
Potters Bar to Cambridge D 70 8
Princes Risborough - BL to D 05 0
Princes Risborough to Banbury C 85 7

R

Railways to Victory C 16 1
Reading to Basingstoke B 27 5
Reading to Didcot C 79 6
Reading to Guildford A 47 5
Redhill to Ashford A 73 4
Return to Blaenau 1970-82 C 64 2
Rhyl to Bangor F 15 4
Rhymney & New Tredegar Lines E 48 2
Rickmansworth to Aylesbury D 61 6
Romania & Bulgaria NG E 23 9
Romneyrail C 32 1
Ross-on-Wye - BLs around E 30 7
Ruabon to Barmouth E 84 0
Rugby to Birmingham E 37 6
Rugby to Loughborough F 12 3
Rugby to Stafford F 07 9
Rugeley to Stoke-on-Trent F 90 1
Ryde to Ventnor A 19 2

S

Salisbury to Westbury B 39 8
Sardinia and Sicily Narrow Gauge F 50 5
Saxmundham to Yarmouth C 69 7
Saxony & Baltic Germany Revisited F 71 0
Saxony Narrow Gauge D 47 0
Seaton & Sidmouth - BLs to A 95 6
Selsey - Branch Line to A 04 8
Sheerness - Branch Line to B 16 2
Shenfield to Ipswich E 96 3
Shrewsbury - Branch Line to A 86 4
Shrewsbury to Chester E 70 3
Shrewsbury to Crewe F 48 2
Shrewsbury to Ludlow E 21 5
Shrewsbury to Newtown E 29 1
Sierra Leone Narrow Gauge D 28 9
Sirhowy Valley Line E 12 3
Sittingbourne to Ramsgate A 90 1
Skegness & Mablethorpe - BL to F 84 0
Slough to Newbury C 56 7
South African Two-foot gauge E 51 2
Southampton to Bournemouth A 42 0
Southend & Southminster BLs E 76 5
Southern Alpine Narrow Gauge F 22 2
Southern France Narrow Gauge C 47 5
South London Line B 46 6
South Lynn to Norwich City F 03 1
Southwold - Branch Line to A 15 4
Spalding - Branch Lines around E 52 9
Spalding to Grimsby F 65 9 6
Stafford to Chester F 34 5

Stafford to Wellington F 59 8
St Albans to Bedford D 08 1
St. Austell to Penzance C 67 3
St. Boswell to Berwick F 44 4
Steaming Through Isle of Wight A
Steaming Through West Hants A 6
Stourbridge to Wolverhampton E 1
St. Pancras to Barking D 68 5
St. Pancras to Folkestone E 88 8
St. Pancras to St. Albans C 78 9
Stratford to Cheshunt F 53 6
Stratford-u-Avon to Birmingham D
Stratford-u-Avon to Cheltenham C
Sudbury - Branch Lines to F 19 2
Surrey Narrow Gauge C 87 1
Sussex Narrow Gauge C 68 0
Swaffham - Branch Lines around F
Swanage to 1999 - BL to A 33 8
Swanley to Ashford B 45 9
Swansea - Branch Lines around F
Swansea to Carmarthen E 59 8
Swindon to Bristol C 96 3
Swindon to Gloucester D 46 3
Swindon to Newport D 30 2
Swiss Narrow Gauge C 94 9

T

Talyllyn 60 E 98 7
Tamworth to Derby F 76 5
Taunton to Barnstaple B 60 2
Taunton to Exeter C 82 6
Taunton to Minehead F 39 0
Tavistock to Plymouth B 88 6
Tenterden - Branch Line to A 21 5
Three Bridges to Brighton A 35 2
Tilbury Loop C 86 4
Tiverton - BLs around C 62 8
Tivetshall to Beccles D 41 8
Tonbridge to Hastings A 44 4
Torrington - Branch Lines to B 37 4
Tourist Railways of France G 04 3
Towcester - BLs around E 39 0
Tunbridge Wells BLs A 32 1

U

Upwell - Branch Line to B 64 0
Uttoxeter to Macclesfield G 05 0

V

Victoria to Bromley South A 98 7
Victoria to East Croydon A 40 6
Vivarais Revisited E 08 6

W

Walsall Routes F 45 1
Wantage - Branch Line to D 25 8
Wareham to Swanage 50 yrs D098
Waterloo to Windsor A 54 3
Waterloo to Woking A 38 3
Watford to Leighton Buzzard D 45 6
Wellingborough to Leicester F 73 4
Welshpool to Llanfair E 49 9
Wenford Bridge to Fowey C 09 3
Westbury to Bath B 55 8
Westbury to Taunton C 76 5
West Cornwall Mineral Rlys D 48 7
West Croydon to Epsom B 08 4
West German Narrow Gauge D 95 9
West London - BLs of C 50 5
West London Line B 84 8
West Wiltshire - BLs of D 12 8
Weymouth - BLs A 65 9
Willesden Jn to Richmond B 71 8
Wimbledon to Beckenham C 58 1
Wimbledon to Epsom B 62 6
Wimborne - BLs around A 97 0
Wisbech - BLs around C 01 7
Witham & Kelvedon - BLs a E 82 (
Woking to Alton A 59 8
Woking to Portsmouth A 25 3
Woking to Southampton A 55 0
Wolverhampton to Shrewsbury E4
Wolverhampton to Stafford F 79 6
Worcester to Birmingham D 97 5
Worcester to Hereford D 38 8
Worthing to Chichester A 06 2
Wrexham to New Brighton E 42
Wroxham - BLs around F 31 4

Y

Yeovil - 50 yrs change C 38 3
Yeovil to Dorchester A 76 5
Yeovil to Exeter A 91 8
York to Scarborough F 23 5

9